Copyright © 2021 by Williams Commerce

Visit The Black Store

8616 Cullen Blvd.
Houston, Texas
77051

theblackstoreinc.com | ourblackslate.com

The Black Store

Lloyd C. Ford II | Tamani A.M. Mwandani

ISBN: 978-1-7366637-0-7

Williams Commerce, LLC

williamscommerce1.com

Table of Contents

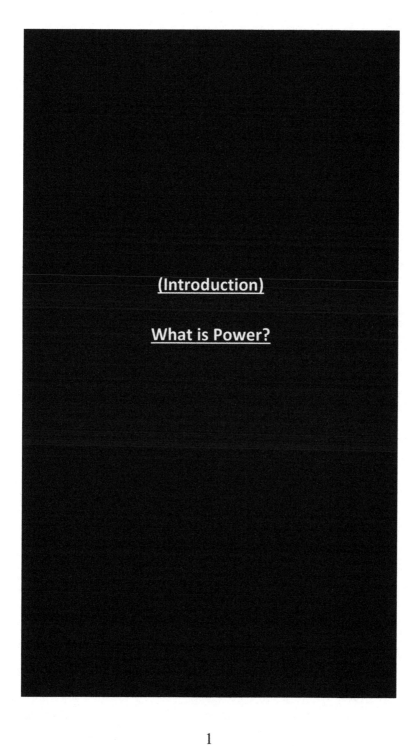

(Introduction)

What is Power?

Power has various and conflicting interpretations; it is like a chameleon; it takes on the texture of its environment. According to *(Dr. Amos Wilson), power* refers to the ability to do, the ability to be, and the ability to prevail. Power is self-realization and self-actualization, and the fulfillment of potential or possibilities. It is essential to our existence and the most influential factor in determining our quality of life, there is no escaping its presence in some form either by others or alternative methods. To deny the presence of power in our lives is to our own peril, there can be detrimental and beneficial aspects of power that can be utilized to achieve personal, social, political and material ends if developed, organized and applied appropriately.

We lack the power and organization to prevent oppression in the Black community. Therefore, Our Black Agenda will lay the foundation of education for issues facing Black communities, educate readers on holding the right elected officials accountable for decisions made in Black communities, and give solutions for issues for Black citizens to apply in their everyday lives to combat institutionalized power against Black people. We will discuss various systems, strategies and techniques that are used to oppress Black people such as, the education system, justice system, community health, community engagement/politics, economic development/opportunity, and community housing. These systems have all been used to work against the best interest of our communities. We will discuss how to advocate and who to hold accountable for these ongoing issues as well as, what to do as individuals to aid in the power of Black people wherever we are. These problems are issues of oppressed Black people, not only in America, but all over the world, and the key to our freedom lies in the future of the steps we take today.

This book will explain how the various systems in America have set up a course of destruction in the Black community and not only blames, but prosecutes the people within them for the condition they are in. Furthermore, it will ask you a series of questions that will educate you on your city or state structure and it will explain how the setup of this system does not serve our best interest because there is no law or any amount of voting alone that will get us out. As we have been shown through history here in America, the laws are only as good as the people who enforce them, and if they choose not to enforce them, we are powerless as a people to stop it. We do not believe having black people inside of the government structure will protect us from oppression, but many of those individuals were educated and put in place by that very system and will not always act in the best interest of themselves. We must act in the best interest of Black people and that begins with every individual taking personal accountability for being a part of the fight and acting in the best interest of Black people.

What is "The Art of Domination"?

Domination is exercising the power in ruling; dominion; supremacy; authority over another. This country uses domination to project its collective will, consciousness, self-image, values, and ideals on Black people as a legitimate representative of the whole societal personality. It seeks to use mechanisms like denial, deception, distortion, and repression to impose its mental and material control on Black people. This is required to maintain power and regulatory dominance of the national and international society, and projects its identity as legitimate and God-given. The perpetual domination of Black people by this nation requires the criminalization of Black people even in circumstances where they have not been identified as having committed, apprehended for, or convicted of a crime. Crime is emphasized in Black communities in order to excuse the over policing of our communities and ultimately the over imprisonment of Black men and women. Domination has justified the criminalization of Black people and manipulated us and others in believing these claims are lawful when, in actuality, the system has created the criminalization of our people and the punishment that allows them to be subjugated to modern day slavery. We often mention the issues of crime in Black communities, but rarely, if ever, talk about the system that actively provokes criminalization and creates the need to perceive Black people as criminals by nature. Once we understand the levers that control criminalization, we will recognize the system isn't created or willing to develop a path of true freedom and equality, and that it feeds off of the demise of Black people and Black communities. We are in a vicious cycle that can only be broken by understanding, seeking and maintaining power of our own through collective organizing around these issues and developing our own solutions. The united states prison system was created and is maintained by our tax dollars, so in a since, we are funding our own oppression through the method of just paying taxes. Major structural changes do not happen overnight or without considerable pressure or force from an opposite party, and power is never given or shared, only taken. Domination is an ongoing tactic to further the subjugation and exploitation of Black people and is sometimes manifested and described as Black on Black crime. The only way for America to maintain and protect its self-image, material wealth, power, and political advantages is to deny truth and reality when it comes to Black people. The reality is that this country could not be possible without the criminalization and subjugation of

Black people. Every industry we lack participation in allows for other people to profit from our demise.

1. What are some of the areas that you think Black people are being systematically/systemically oppressed?

_____

_____

_____

_____

_____

_____

The SWOT Analysis

Understanding what it means to be Black where you live.

If one were to add up all the years of everything Black people have been through since the first slave ship arrived on the shores of North America in 1619, it would total over 3,000 years of assault, terror and destruction. Everything that's been done to Black people has been done on purpose. We have endured over 3,000 years of continuous, relentless, methodical, intentional, simultaneous, systematic and unapologetic anti-Black acts of terror. No people have gone through what we've gone and lived to talk about it. When Europeans arrived on the shores of North America, there were over 500 Native American Nations. Where is that 500 now???

Black people are born into a war we did not start, we're surround on every front and we're over 350 years behind on *preparing* to fight back. No war has ever been won without intelligence, data and information and this war that our people are born into is no different.

We cannot win without intelligence, data and information!

Understanding the SWOT Analysis

A SWOT Analysis (**S**trengths, **W**eakness, **O**pportunities & **T**hreats) is a *very specific and detailed* document most commonly found and used in the business world to determine the viability of a new business, product or service offering to a specific target market before bringing it to market. The document is designed to not only answer the basic question of "Is this a good idea to do what we're thinking about doing?" but also, after the decision has been made to move forward with the production of that idea, give a detailed analysis of what the new product/service may face and ultimately deal with over a period of time.

Our SWOT analysis for the purpose of this book and Black empowerment is *not* about a new business, product or service, but a much more critical and important task: the overall survival and forward progress of Black people. Although you don't need a group of people to create the SWOT analysis, it is highly recommended that you find a group to do so because different people are going to have a different perspective on the issues Black people are facing in your town/city and that different perspective is very important and very useful.

Within the pages of this book, you're going to find a number of questions relating to different subject matters in the political realm that are designed to not just educate you, but to also give you the tools that you need to mobilize and organize your community and subsequently move forward after doing so. The SWOT analysis will make it easier to mobilize and organize because you'll have a blueprint as to what's at your disposal, per Black people in your town/city, by which you can use to start creating the kind of change our people need.

Creating Your SWOT Analysis

Strengths

Where are Black people **strong** where you live? What are the positives that Black people bring to the table in your town/city that can be used to create change?

A few examples of where Black people could be **strong** are.

- **Leadership** – If you have people who have working to help the community for a long time

- **Resources** – If, due to business or geographic location, Black people have access to resources (man-made, government or natural) to help them in their daily lives

- **Industries** – If one or several industries exist that employ a large number of Black people

- **Population** – If there are a large number of Black people in your town/city

These are all just examples. The **Strengths** part of your SWOT analysis should be MUCH longer than four (4) items.

Weaknesses

- Where are Black people **weak** where you live? What areas in your town/city can Black people improve?
- A few examples of where Black people could be **weak** are...
- **Black Owned Businesses** – Do Black people have a small number of Black owned businesses in your area (1 person business entities should NOT be counted)?

- **Income** – Is income for a large number of Black people low. Is poverty a serious issue for Black people where you live?

- **Crime** – Is crime high and if so, what areas/sectors (youth, murders, human trafficking, etc...) are they high?

- **Political Representation** – Do the majority (grassroots) of Black people have strong political representation? Don't confuse "strong representation" with melanin (dark skin) content. Everyone who has melanin isn't automatically an ally.

These are all just examples. The **Weakness** part of your SWOT analysis should be MUCH longer than four (4) items.

NOTE: Most weakness can also be opportunities as well as threats.

Opportunities

What specific **opportunities** exist for Black people where you live? What areas in your town/city can Black people find to help them improve their condition?

A few examples of what **opportunities** might look like for Black people are...

- **Inexpensive Land** – Is land inexpensive to purchase or widely available where you live?

- **Abandoned Buildings** – Are there a large number of abandoned buildings where you live OR structures that are available for rent or lease?

- **Consciousness** – Is there a high level of consciousness among Black people where you live? Does your town/city have a long track record of Black people mobilizing and organizing for the betterment of the Black community?

- **Racial Barriers** – Are the "Barriers to Entry" relatively low as it relates to opportunities (business, resources, grants) where you live for Black people?

These are all just examples. The **Opportunities** part of your SWOT analysis should be MUCH longer than four (4) items.

NOTE: Several opportunities can be capitalized on and taken advantage of with your strengths list if properly vetted, organized and used.

Threats

What specific **threats** exist for Black people where you live? What are the dangers to/for Black people in your town/city that can/do specifically jeopardize the lives of Black people (immediate or long term)?

A few examples of what the **threats** might look like for Black people are…

- **Police Brutality** – Is police brutality particularly high for Black people in your town/city?

- **Corrupt Politicians** – Are there a large number of corrupt politicians in the town/city where you live?

- **Gang Activity** – Are gangs a major issue for Black people where you live?

- **School to Prison Pipeline** – Is "School to Prison Pipeline" activity particularly high where you live? A poor education system, economic system and hyperactive police/criminal justice element all play a key role in this particular threat. If the previous statement is true, the S2P Pipeline is, more than likely, alive, well and very active for Black children and people in your area.

These are all just examples. The **Threats** part of your SWOT analysis should be MUCH longer than four (4) items.

NOTE: Most threats are also weakness.

The SWOT Analysis is an excellent tool that should be completed before progressing further. Understanding the landscape where we live and how we can us what we already have to better positions ourselves and other like-minded Brothers & Sisters is an absolute must.

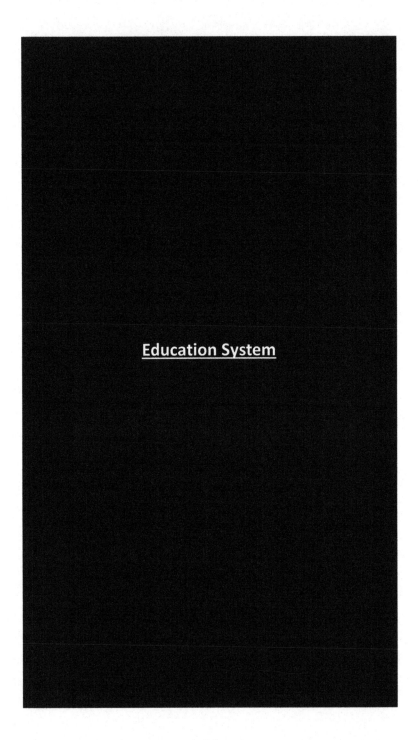

Education System

The public-school system has failed the Black community by not preparing our kids for the world they will soon be adults in. A few key issues with the public school system are school funding and how they qualify schools to receive funds based on the states standardized test in most states, unequal resources among schools that leave Black schools behind lacking critical resources, the exploitation of the special education program being used to set Black kids on a course of failure, out of date and unrelatable curriculums that don't engage Black kids or equip them with the tools they will need as Black men and women to act in the best interest of their own people, the school to prison pipeline that funnels our people into a modern day slave industry, and equal qualifications for teachers in schools that receive public dollars. We must be involved in every decision made about the education system and hold all elected officials accountable for the decisions made or not made in the best interest of Black people. We must also create our own curriculums for our culture and the problems we face today to empower the next generation to act in the best interest of Black people in the future. Holding the leaders accountable is just the first step, we must take personal accountability by attending public meetings pertaining to education, join education groups seeking system transformation, and other efforts to be a part of the process. Education, like every other system plaguing Black people has been politicized to keep us a step behind the ruling class. The studies that tell us about ourselves are funded and enacted by the people that oppress us and we expect them to implement the kind of programs/solutions that will help us defeat the system they set in place. The miseducation of our kids plays a critical role in the economic system of this country; therefore, it is reasonable to assume that we play a role in the prison system, and the school to prison pipeline feeds our children to this system.

1. What are your beliefs about the American Education system?

_____

_____

_____

_____

_____

Public School Funding

There are a few factors in public school funding that are unequal. One factor of this issue is standardized testing; they have used this as a tool to deny schools key funding and Black schools have been faced with closures all over the nation because of this issue. They have condemned Black kids and schools over standardized tests, and we have verifiable proof that the public education system does not equip most Black schools with the proper tools and books to prepare for the test. Therefore, creating the conditions for our schools to most likely fail and be subjected to closing. Or, being taken over by outside educational groups that signifies less community ability and allows for less control. Current school systems create the bad learning environment and the conditions for failure, then use those conditions to close Black schools for bad performance.

In states like Texas, teachers are not allowed to strike according to the contract they sign for employment which also deters them from speaking out on key issues. The state guarantees every district a certain amount of funding for each student, but the inequity lies in yet another factor that fuels school funding and that is property taxes. By using property taxes for funding in select districts, funding will always be unequal due to a large amount of Black public schools are located in poor Black neighborhoods inundated with churches that don't contribute to taxable income of the community.

Black people are majority renters with little ownership of our communities and not large contributors to the tax base of our local economy. We must advocate that school funding not depend on standardized testing, but other metrics that do not exclude Black communities for being poor.

Our own investigation must be done on the breakdown of funding going to every school, and what lever stops our schools from being properly and equitably funded and where are our funds being allocated. We must question the high wages of educational leaders who do not serve a real purpose in the education of our kids and redirect those funds toward the more motivated teachers in our Black schools.

Special Education Exploitation

Special education is a program that is supposed to identify and give specialized instruction to kids with autism, who are emotionally disturbed, dyslexic and, the most common used term today "ADHD" which cannot be proven scientifically, among many other disabilities.

It is another public-school program setup to help but missed the mark and allows room for exploitation of the most underserved communities which are majority Black. Public schools have begun to use special education as a revenue source, rather than an opportunity to offer students in need the extra resources they need to become better. Instead, special education, has become a lifetime label of no accountability or low expectations for the student and a permanent increase in government funding for the school. This incentivizes schools to increase the classification of the number of students in special education programs with no motivation to help the student's overall performance without decreasing funding for the school.

We must demand measures are put in place to stop the exploitation of this program for additional funding, which sets our kids up to be stigmatized and marginalized through the education system. We must demand full transparency and updated reports from schools regarding the decrease of students in "special education" programs. A great number of students that spend their entire public education in this program serves to feed the school to prison pipeline. We must question any diagnosis given to us by black or white professionals who have been taught, educated and/or trained in this system because they have been taught to uphold the same miseducation and unscientific diagnosis like ADHD, which is used to prescribe our kids unnecessary medication for a condition that is only "proven" by the opinion of a professional taught by the system and to uphold that system.

School To Prison Pipeline

A great number of students that spend their entire public education in this program has feed the school to prison pipeline. The school-to-prison pipeline is a process through which students are pushed out of schools and into the city's criminal justice system. It is a process of criminalizing youth and is carried out by disciplinary policies and practices within schools that put students into contact with law enforcement. Once they are put into contact with law enforcement for disciplinary reasons, many are then pushed out of the educational environment and into the juvenile and criminal justice environment and system for minor mistakes. The key policies and practices that created and now maintain the school-to-prison pipeline include zero tolerance policies that mandate harsh punishments for both minor and major infractions, exclusion of students from schools through punitive suspensions and expulsions, and the presence of police on campus as school resource officers. These policies and practices became common following a deadly spate of school shootings across the U.S. in the 1990s. These shootings did not happen at Black schools but was used to place a police presence at our schools in order to subjugate our kids to the criminal justice system and set them on a course for legalized slavery known to us as the US Penal System.

The system has found many ways to criminalize Blackness and is evidenced through the increase of a large police presence in our Black schools. We must demand an end to zero tolerance policies that have done more harm than good on effective ways to discipline Black children. We must implement procedures to discipline students within the public-school system that does not displace our children disproportionately to other races.

We must allow kids to make mistakes without the fear of going to jail or long-term probation for minor offenses. Black children should not have to start the process of punishment as if they are going to court like in a criminal proceeding. We must understand that the destruction of Black youth brings billions of dollars to the structure of this country. It is in the best interest of the structure for these systems to continue as they are induced for political and economic purposes.

Updated School Curriculum

Public-school curriculums today are introduced to prepare students for the states standardize testing at the end of each year. It has only served the purpose to punish Black schools with closure and take over with no local supervision. This system of learning does not prepare our kids for the world they will be facing or allow them to function at a high level and have presence and pride in the corporate job structure but sets them on a path to be menial/manual workers of society and not creators of their own destiny.

School curriculums should be relevant to everyday society and how to think outside of the box, but instead they are condensed subjects that are rarely used in life and does not educate them to how the system actually works and the levers to seek change in the areas that don't serve Black people. Schools must relate math lessons as it relates to business and financial literacy, accurate accounts of history so that the past is not repeated, and other life related subjects that will ensure Black students understand this capitalistic system and our place as Black people in it.

We must demand that all school curriculums are continuously updated and reviewed by parents and other community education advocates to ensure academic relevance. We cannot just expect through advocation alone a school curriculum will be developed or implemented to help us maneuver this system. Instead, we must learn to gain the most relevant skills that we can apply to today's world and seek ways to implement them in our communities. We must prepare our kids for the needs of the Black community and instill in them the pride and confidence to bring those skills back to the community and increase our economic power. The current curriculum prepares Black kids to serve the needs of others and give the perception that being successful lies outside of the community they live in. Other races send their kids to college on the economics we provide from the businesses they open in our communities, but in actuality we should reap the benefits of our dollars and we are more likely to reinvest those dollars back into Black communities. This shows how education itself play a critical role in the economics within our own communities and can be a powerful tool to our survival as a people.

Each one of these topics are important in the education of Black children. We must demand a change to how school funds are allocated to schools, the end of the exploitation of the special education program that sets our kids on a path of destruction, the end of the school to prison pipeline activity that prosecutes kids for minor mistakes and introduce them to the justice system, and the modernization of curriculums being studied by our kids that are relevant for them to succeed and become productive in the Black community. These things alone will not be accomplished simply by advocating or demanding, we must individually put in the time and work to bring about change in the education system whether we have kids attending public school or not. We must be willing to be a part of the process by showing up for local education meetings, joining education groups and other local efforts that we deem effective, and be willing to call out local officials when our needs are not met. At public meetings, many decisions are made without the presence of the community they are residing over. We must make time out of our busy lives to begin to address these issues in our communities or we find ourselves powerless when things don't happen. We can no longer be complacent in our communities, but act with proactiveness and purpose on the future we want for our kids.

1. What are your beliefs about the American Education system?

_____

_____

_____

_____

_____

2. Who is on your city/county/parish School Board and what areas do they represent?

_____

_____

_____

_____

_____

3. When are school board meetings held?

_____

_____

_____

_____

_____

_____

4. When is the next school board election?

_____

_____

_____

_____

_____

_____

5. Who controls property taxes in your city/county/parish, what kind of job are they doing ("Good", "Bad", etc.) and when is this person up for reelection?

_____

_____

_____

_____

_____

6. Who ran against this person during the last election and why?

_____

_____

_____

_____

_____

7. Who is in charge of your city/county/parish's school district special education funding and is it being used properly?

_____

_____

_____

_____

_____

8. Who ran against the person in charge of special education funding and why?

_____

_____

_____

_____

_____

9. Who is in charge of your city/county/parish's juvenile justice/criminalization area and how many children have THEY sent to prison OR placed on the path to go to prison?

_____

_____

_____

_____

_____

10. Who ran against the person in charge of area and why?

_____

_____

_____

_____

_____

11. What Black child advocacy groups exist in your city/county/parish and when do they meet?

_____

_____

_____

_____

_____

12. Per the opening question for this section and what you have just learned from reading it, can you do more to assist the Black community in this area? If so, in detail, what can you do?

_____

_____

_____

_____

_____

Action Steps

Attend School Board / District Meetings

1. School district meetings are held in every city to update and get the communities opinion on decisions being made. Attending these meeting will allow us to be proactive instead of reactive when bad decisions are made. Just attending the meeting will not always get us the outcome we may be looking for, but it allows us to identify school officials that are acting against and/or for our best interest.

Identify All Education Leaders

2. We must identify all elected officials who make decisions about our education system to evaluate if they are acting in the best interest of the Black community. We should hold them accountable for full transparency of decisions being made in the community they serve. If they do not have a consistent community meeting or avenue to communicate information, we should demand one.

Find Local Grassroot Organizations To Partner With

3. We must always seek out like minded allies in the issues that plague our people. This task is too big to take on alone, and there is no individualistic goal outside of group work that will be more effective in our fight for Black people. We must join all organizations that say they speak on behalf of our people and challenge any actions that do not speak to the root of our issues. We must find more reasons to work together rather than not work together, and we must not let things like religious ideology or political propaganda prevent our partnership to bring about change in our Black communities.

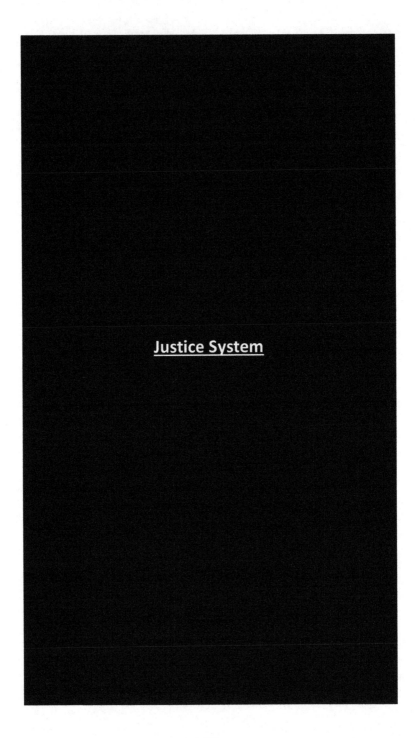

Justice System

The Criminal Justice system has treated Black people unfairly since its founding and has managed to incarcerate more Black people (based on our percentage of the overall population) than any other race living in America. We are sentenced longer than any other group for the same or lesser crimes committed regardless of criminal background. Our neighborhoods have been over policed to persecute Black people with mental or drug issues who need medical help and not jail time. We have also been killed at higher rates by police officers without any law enforcement "professionals" being prosecuted, therefore killing Black men and women with impunity. These issues continuously happen and leave black people feeling powerless. We must demand full transparency and compliance from police departments on police involved killings of Black people, publicly elected community oversight boards that review all police involved violence, the end of felony disenfranchisement that prohibits convicted felons from voting and other rights of this country. The transformation of the prison system that institutionalize Black men and women for mainly nonviolent offences that will set them back should also be done Even among their exit of the system as second-class citizens, re-entry services for prisoners should be evaluated and utilized to not only help them back into society but to prevent them from being reoffenders. Just being advocates for issues in our system is not enough. We must identify all elected officials that make decisions on the justice system and research what solutions they are implementing to make a sustainable change. We must identify all law enforcement that patrol our communities to ensure we know who to hold accountable when issues occur. Laws set in place like qualified immunity, which gives police officers the license to kill without proper accountability for their actions. Lack of opportunity is one of the main components to the crime rate in our Black communities, so if we increase the opportunities, it will immediately affect the crime rate.

1. What are your beliefs about the Criminal Justice system?

_____

_____

_____

_____

_____

_____

Police Accountability/Transparency

Many of the police department budgets in major cities across the country have grown to over a billion dollars per year and is steadily rising with the increase of advanced technology and a variety of assault weapons to use on Black people and communities where we are already over policed and persecuted. Police are rarely, if ever, prosecuted for the atrocities committed against the Black community and in order to maintain police transparency, we must demand police cam footage be released in a certain timeframe regardless of investigation status, public access to police complaints and/or records similar to other public agencies. We must demand copies of yearly detailed budgets of how all public dollars are being spent within the police department, and all asset forfeitures of individuals that have not been charged with a crime they take advantage of each year. The local police department should share all information with the Community Oversight Board to make a determination that would be shared with the public beyond the typical police version of events that always seems to justify the killing of an unarmed person. These changes will not come easy, but each one of these leaders making these decisions are elected by the community and these things should play a part in them keeping their job. We should negotiate the contract with the police union every few years depending on the charter of our cities; this is when new amendments of the process and how it relates to the community should be pushed for change in order for the contract to be renewed. We must use all avenues to accomplish our goals to protect ourselves and our communities and take control of the entities that are funded by our tax dollars. These accountability measures along with actions on the ground will help us get one step closer to holding police accountable for killing unarmed Black people in this country.

Community Oversight Board

The community oversight board (often referred to as a civilian oversight or review board) is intended to give the community an inside voice on police involved issues that traditionally have excluded the community from knowing any information until the police have crafted their narrative that best suits their needs to justify a given situation. The issue with most of these boards is that they are selected by city officials who do not have the community's best interest at heart but intend to play the same political game as the police department by concealing evidence from the public. The community oversight board must be free from corruption and strings to maintain its unbiased decisions in these situations. For example, local review boards such as in the City of Houston are selected and approved by the mayor and city council. This process is a direct conflict of interest because the same people making these decisions have historically voted against any community lead initiatives to bring real change. Cities that have citizen review boards are mainly ineffective because of the selection process and the requirements it takes to be considered to sit on the board. The Community Oversight board in the city of Houston requires them to report their findings to the mayor, chief of police, and public safety committee before sharing them with the community, which does the community a major injustice. This allows city officials to manipulate the decisions of the board before they reach the community which allows for deception and the lack of accountability to continue. We must fight for a true independent community board whose main priority and allegiance lies with the community it is intended to serve. The board should be elected publicly by the community and not selected by the mayor, city council, or any other political entity.

Equal Sentencing

It has been proven that Black people receive longer jail time than any other race for similar crimes committed by other groups. This disparity causes Black people to serve double sometimes triple jail/prison sentences in the same courtroom and sentenced by the same judge. The system prosecuting drugs that are known to be used in Black communities should not be qualified to prosecute by more severe measures. For example, crack cocaine, which is commonly used in Black communities, carries a penalty that is 100 times more severe than cocaine, which is more common by white people or individuals with higher incomes. There have been measures implemented such as the Fair Sentencing Act in 2010 which was intended to bring the disparity in drug sentencing from 100:1 to 18:1, that is just one example of how Black people are unfairly treated and why we are the dominant population in the prison system. This is just another example of our powerlessness to choose our own future in this nation and have equal protections under the law unless we begin to search for and obtain our own power. These disparities will continue to happen until we have power of our own to stop them which starts with gaining our own political power to put an end to harsh sentencing for Black people. Instead of long sentences, we can repeal the

"Truth in Sentencing" and "Three-Strikes" laws. Furthermore, we can repeal mandatory minimums, use alternatives to incarceration, prohibit incarceration for failure to appear, revise sentencing guidelines, and elect our own judges that will rule in our favor for local decisions. To gain the power to affect real change in equal sentencing, we must acquire our own political power through grassroots mobilizing, organizing and controlling our local politics.

Felony Disenfranchisement

Over 6 million people are disenfranchised due to a felony conviction. These individuals are under continuous supervision and the numbers have risen over recent years. These citizens have served their time, (many for non-violent offenses) but are largely still unable to exercise their rights to vote for elected officials. Felony disenfranchisement varies from state to state, some states restore rights after the sentence has been completed, a few states never restore voting rights, and some states select who can vote and who cannot. Felony disenfranchisement goes beyond the voting rights of felons, but also includes being excluded from housing and job opportunities that require employers to know the status of your criminal history. Regardless if an offense was non-violent in nature or happened many years ago which is majority of the cases, this affects Black people more than any other race because we do not own most of the real estate to house our own people or our own companies to offer our people job opportunities. This system has been used to exclude and revoke the rights of individuals who have been incarcerated from decent places to live in certain areas, choosing who represents your rights in public office, and employment opportunities that pay a livable wage to prevent repeat offenders. The system does more harm by making it harder for individuals just exiting the prison system who most likely need the most help, instead it increases their chances to become repeat offenders. This system is maintained because it is economically profitable for America. Corporations make millions per year from our tax dollars for monitoring prisoners once they are released from incarceration. This is just one example of how we are funding our own oppression under this system. We pay the politicians to pass laws that incarcerate us, and our tax dollars pay the prison to house us. We then pay the probation employees and services to monitor us once we have paid our debt to society. Until we understand that we hold the power to our own oppression, we will continue to feel and be powerless; but when that power is realized, each individual can understand the role we all need to play to be totally and completely free.

Correctional Re-Entry Services

Correctional re-entry services are intended to help offenders rebuild their lives and re-enter their communities. Through services such as literacy training, housing location, alcohol and substance comprehensive treatment and case management, offenders gain much needed skills and are empowered to succeed.

This program rarely takes root in a large capacity in Black communities due to intentional obstacles like funding and public opinion of this type of housing in certain communities. We should embrace these types of effective programs to help the majority of Black people being imprisoned to reduce the overall amount of people who end up back in prison.

Some of these individuals can be empowered to be leaders in the Black community and steer others in the right direction. We must do more than just demand opportunities for felons, but also be open to hiring and giving Black felons a second chance when we hold the power to do so.

We must have a deeper understanding for individuals that have been caught up in the system; without condoning the mistakes they have made. These are Black people that have the potential to be productive in our society and give back to our social system. Most of these individuals will only get a fair chance in Black communities and we must have the opportunities for them in our own communities.

What Do We Need To Do?

The American justice system is the largest in the world with over 2 million individuals incarcerated in federal, state, or local prisons and jails. Black people are 5.9 times likely to be incarcerated than white people. The United States operates two distinct criminal justice systems: one for wealthy people and another for poor people. These disparities do not change unless we apply deliberate action to acquire our own power in this country to transform the justice system beginning on a local level. We all must be a part of effective organizations to bring about change in our Black communities and we must constantly evaluate our efforts to maintain that we are dealing with the root of the issue and treating the symptoms.

1. Who is the "Top Cop" (Sheriff, Chief, etc.) in your city/county/parish? Who ran against them and why?

_____

_____

_____

_____

_____

2. What is your city's/county's/parish's position and/or police on community ran review boards for police killings? If one exists, who runs it and how does it work? If one does not exist, why not?

_____

_____

_____

_____

_____

3. What is your city's/county's/parish's position and/or policy on "Felony Disenfranchisement"? If they do not have one, how can one be started?

_____

_____

_____

_____

_____

4. What is your city's/county's/parish's position and/or policy on "Community Reentry Programs" for those recently released from jail/prison? How does this program/policy work, is it sufficient and how can it be made better?

_____

_____

_____

_____

_____

5. What is your city's/county's/parish's position and/or policy on "Qualified Immunity?"

_____

_____

_____

_____

_____

6. What is your city's/county's/parish's position and/or policy on asset forfeitures of people who have not been charged with a crime?

_____

_____

_____

_____

_____

7. Does a Law Enforcement Community Oversight board exist for your city/county/parish? If so, how does it work. If not, why not?

_____

_____

_____

_____

_____

8. Per the opening question for this section and what you have just learned from reading it, can you do more to assist the Black community in this area? If so, in detail, what can you do?

_____

_____

_____

_____

_____

Action Steps

Identify Elected Officials

1. County elected officials play a valuable role in the criminal justice system, they pass ordinances, establish policies, selecting administrators and staff, set public safety priorities, and make funding decisions that impact the system directly and indirectly. We must identify all decision makers in our Black communities to hold them accountable for the lack of progress in the justice system. These individuals are elected by the public but rarely serve the needs of Black people.

- Acquire baseline data on the justice system.
- Identify justice system stakeholders.
- Identify opportunities for improvement.
- Demand updates of improvements.

Identify Local Justice Groups

2. We must get involved in grassroots efforts to bring about change in our communities, we must identify all groups working around us to evaluate the steps being made. There are no individual efforts that any of us can take that will bring about sufficient change for our communities, therefore, group organizations that understand the true revolutionary nature that needs to take place as discussed in this book are of critical importance.

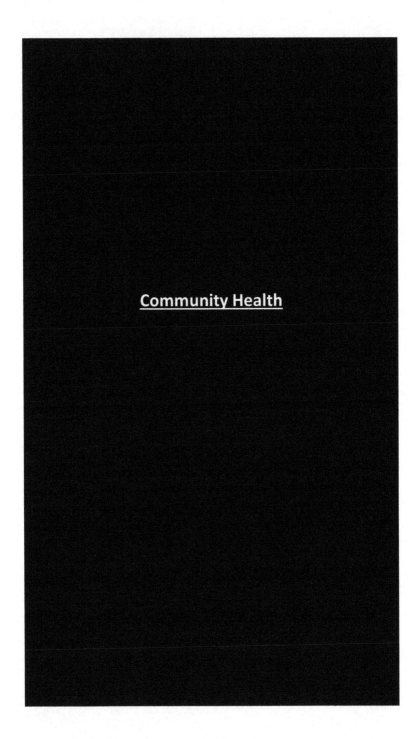

Community Health

Community health examines the health status of a defined group of people, or community, and the actions and conditions that protect and improve the health of the community. Community health can include a wide range of solutions that deal with multiple entities that have no communication between one another. Alcoholism and drug abuse are some of the leading factors to homelessness, that is not to exclude mental health and other underlying issues.

Black communities have a shortage of healthy food options and are plagued with fast food restaurants, liquor stores, and other unhealthy choices, we must use city ordinances and other tools to reverse negative effects on our communities. Our communities are filled with contaminated water sources that causes cancer, mental health problems, and other issues. Cities like Flint, Michigan have been devastated and left with no clean running water and must fulfill all their needs with bottled water, but contaminated water in our poor communities is not an isolated occurrence.

We must demand better and take personal accountability to solve these ongoing issues, we must work with schools, civic groups, nonprofit organizations, doctors, mental health professionals, employers, and other community institutions that have the tools to aid our communities with these problems. We can no longer treat the symptoms of the broader problem without addressing the root economic issues and sustainable solutions that can be supported by the communities they intend to serve.

In our demand to change our communities, we can't expect full cooperation from the political structure until we control the politician or create the policy that holds the reigns to some of the resources to aid in these issues. Our community deficiencies serve the system economically by using this to increase police budgets and funnel black people into the prison system, and we fund the whole operation with our tax dollars.

While participating in the political process, we must understand the development of our own institutions and health solutions will be key to healing our communities. If we are overly dependent on other people for the health of our communities, we will always be unsatisfied with the outcome and results.

1. What are your beliefs about the overall health of the Black community in your city/county/parish?

_____

_____

_____

_____

_____

_____

Community Health Choices

Quality healthcare institutions are hard to find in most Black communities and millions go without health insurance, which makes this task harder to bring quality options and/or solutions to. Our dependence on government entities has failed us because we lack representation interest and commitment to the Black community and a lack of tax dollars allocated towards lower income communities because they do not control the levers to hold elected officials accountable. Most quality healthcare institutions are outside Black communities and largely out of reach for the majority of its residents because we do not hold the political or economic power to create the change we need. We must demand that our tax dollars are spent in ways that will bring more quality healthcare institutions to Black communities as well as addressing access to these institutions for uninsured residents. Advocating and voting for certain representatives only gets us so far. Without first organizing our own power locally, we cannot expect to get what we need by simply asking. We experience disparities in the healthcare industry by race discrimination, misinformation on chronic health issues, access to health care because of lack of funds, mental health, and preventative health screenings. We must begin to support healthy food choices and natural remedies to eliminate the harmful effects of modern medicine and its effects on the body. Most Black communities lack the resources for healthy food choices or healthy institutions, so we must develop these things through partnership with other Black groups and individuals to bring about necessary and needed change.

Alcohol/Drug Abuse/Homelessness

There are a lot of organizations that offer services to Black communities and therefore take in millions of dollars from the government to do so, and the majority of these organizations are white. These organizations made it their life's mission to aid low income communities and, like modern, capitalistically driven, health care systems, they are focused on the treatment with no cure in mind. They continuously use millions of dollars for salaries and holding families in need depending on their next "fix", rather than using those funds to address the root of these issues. We must demand more treatment centers instead of criminalizing individuals that have a problem with alcohol, drug abuse, and other problems that should not be solved with jail time. Instead, public funding must be allocated towards addressing the cause of individuals turning to substance abuse and treatment for those who have fallen short by putting funds towards opportunity that prevents individuals from turning to drugs in the first place. Millions of public funds have been used to aid organizations with no sustainable programs or economic plan for our communities. They have aided our communities to fall further behind without programs to address the lack of opportunity to pull the individual and community out of poverty. By addressing alcoholism and other drug related issues, we can more directly affect the homeless population and the amount of people suffering on the streets to feed their addictions. We must understand these issues will continue to go unsolved by depending on government institutions and private organizations that we did not create or that were created with the wrong premise. These institutions serve the nation's economic needs by employing more cops for Black communities, prosecutors to put Black drug users in jail instead of treatment centers, and more prisons to house Black people for modern day slave labor. Products created by major companies are still being used in our communities and these companies still use prison labor for some of their business operations for a fraction of the price they would have to pay a person in the real working pool. These entities use our own tax dollars to keep us enslaved and take jobs from people that could use those wages to live and avoid drugs, crime, and eventually jail time. Most of the homeless population in Black communities comprise people with drug/ alcohol abuse issues and mental health problems. This is profitable for this nation and maintained by this nation, therefore will never be eliminated without a complete system transformation which does not happen without first obtaining and then exercising power.

Healthy Food Choices/Contaminated Water

Healthy food choices are rare in low-income communities and are replaced by large fast food chains that do not aid the community in healthy food options and only offer minimum wage jobs to the members of that community. Grocery stores in these communities are poorly maintained with limited healthy options that are not Genetically Modified Organism (GMO). Community members are forced to shop at corner stores and dollar stores with cheap versions of so-called household essentials (milk, cheese, packaged meats, etc.) that is not designed to offer the body key daily nutrients. Our community's lack of access to healthy foods did not happen by accident, but a design to hurt Black communities. We must make a conscious decision to bring access to our own neighborhoods by growing our own foods, opening our own food stores, and developing solutions for ourselves. This doesn't mean don't hold local leaders for access to be created through our tax dollars and do their job, for too long we have just asked for what we want instead of using our collective power to create the change we need. We must learn from past interactions that elected officials and voting alone does not work in our favor , and in order to receive the outcomes that serve our communities, we have to have a list of goals for the elected officials and another set of goals for ourselves within the community. Habits are not easily broken, and it will take time to change our taste to a healthier diet. We have been misinformed about health conditions that are prevalent in/with Black people as hereditary, when in fact the only thing that is hereditary are the traditions in the foods we eat and how they are prepared which result in the same health diseases generation after generation.

Clean water is essential for a healthy life, yet Black communities all around the united states are experiencing contaminated water sources. This is a result of decaying pipes, contaminated land of low-income communities and other man-made issues. Contaminated water sources can cause serious health issues in fetal development, other fertility issues, cancer, learning disabilities, nausea, and even death in extreme circumstances. Despite news coverage and the amount of Black people we vote into office every year, these issues remain. Until we decide to better understand how to obtain power and then use that power while also holding our elected officials accountable, these problems will go unresolved and inevitably get worse. This continues to happen to Black housing development because of our powerlessness as a people and the lack of effort we make in organizing for political power. The decisions to build public housing without maintaining safety are made to maximize profits for people and not in the best interest of the families that will be living in it. We must begin to organize politically around what we want, as well as create opportunities in our own communities if we are to be successful.

What Do We Need To Do?

Changing community health standards is challenging as individuals or for one organization, so it takes a collective effort in many different areas to bring about real and lasting change. We must dedicate our time to each one of these problems such as alcoholism, drug abuse, developing healthy food choices in our own communities and demanding more quality healthcare choices to our neighborhoods with the tax dollars we already provide. These issues will not be not solved unless we take personal accountability in the areas we are passionate enough to give our time and efforts to.

We must demand more from our elected officials and their actions within the community and identify Black organizations that are active and working towards solutions. We must not let fear stop us from creating solutions in areas where we see a need and work with other like-minded individuals to create the change we want. Most of these efforts do not take millions of dollars, but just a willingness to act on or within a specific problem and putting actions towards that area.

1. How many quality health institutions are within a 5-mile radius of the Black communities in your city/county/parish?

_____

_____

_____

_____

_____

2. Who is responsible for access to quality health institutions for the Black community in your city/county/parish?

_____

_____

_____

_____

_____

3. After determining who is responsible for access to quality health institutions for the Black community in your city/county/parish, research to see if that was a part of their previous campaign pledge. If so, can you track their progress? If not, why not?

_____

_____

_____

_____

_____

4. What is your city/county/parish's policy of diverting funds from the police department (commonly referred to as "Defunding the Police") to mental health entities who are trained to "deescalate and treating" as opposed to "escalating and harming?"

_____

_____

_____

_____

5. What entities in your city/county/parish currently provide mental health treatment and what are their greatest issues for support and expansion?

_____

_____

_____

_____

_____

6. Are there any Farmers Markets close to the Black Communities in your city/county/parish? If so, how can you help them be/do better? If not, how can you help to get one started?

_____

_____

_____

_____

_____

7. How many urban gardeners and Black farmers exist within a 50-mile radius of the Black community in your city/county/parish and how can the fresh vegetables and fruits they grow be delivered to the community?

_____

_____

_____

_____

_____

8. Did any currently elected official address the Food Desert issue during their election/reelection campaign? If so, what are they doing about it? If not, why not?

_____

_____

_____

_____

_____

9. Did any currently elected official address the clean water issue during their election/reelection campaign? If so, what are they doing about it? If not, why not?

_____

_____

_____

_____

_____

10. Per the opening question for this section and what you've just learned from reading it, can you do more to assist the Black community in this area? If so, in detail, what can you do?

_____

_____

_____

_____

_____

Action Steps

Identify Steps for Elected Officials

1. Identify steps being taken to bring quality healthcare options to your community, identify resources being provided for alcohol/ drug abuse/ homelessness issues in your area, what is being done to eliminate food deserts and over saturation of fast food chains in Black communities.

2. Identify your local public housing authority to investigate deals involving contaminated water/land sources being consumed, and other issues relating to health.

Identify Effective/Ineffective Organizations

3. We must identify organizations that are already doing the work in some of these areas of focus, we must evaluate their short-term and long-term goals and plans for the area they plan to work and/or affect change in.

4. Identify Local Healthy Food Sources/Local Farms Identify local organizations and groups with agriculture programs that can potentially bring solutions to Black communities. We must learn to repeat this process and spread these good programs through all our communities that are experiencing food deserts or limited healthy food options.

Community Housing

Community housing has always been used to control multiple aspects of certain populations of people that either do not own the homes where they live or maintain the political or economic power to stop changes that seek to displace them. Public housing is determined by factors not controlled by Black people and is connected to the schools our children attend, the businesses that surround our communities, and the overall quality of the neighborhood itself and these factors speak to a greater issue. Laws such as the "Community Reinvestment Act" have fallen short because the laws that are enacted are only as good as the people in power's willingness to enforce them. Elected officials over time have shown us that laws alone will not get the job done. The "Community Reinvestment Act" violators, combined with redlining, has restricted bank reinvestment in Black communities and thus created decaying communities without the social structure to rebuild themselves.

A community that is dependent on others to fulfill their everyday needs will never work and will be subjected to the will of others. Public housing was created for individuals and families without local affordable housing options and these type communities can be found in almost every Black community around the nation. Large populations of Black people are dependent on government assistance with no programing to help our people raise themselves out of their current situation and become fully self-sufficient, which is supposed to be a part of the public housing program. We must demand local elected leaders that play a part in the public housing issue show, in grave detail, how taxpayer dollars are being spent for programs that are not producing any results via the reduction of the amount of public housing participants. Instead, each year the budgets grow and the amount of recipients grows with it. We must hold our elected officials accountable for showing the results of millions of dollars being spent with no metrics to track its progress. We must demand transparency in the form of detailed reports on expenditures made with public dollars. In Houston, Texas criminal complaints were filed in 2020 against the Houston Housing Authority for using COVID 19 as a means of hiding records and the misuse of public funds, these practices are taking place by city agencies all over the united states without holding these entities accountable. We can begin to address these issues by taking personal accountability and getting involved in the fight by identifying local leaders in charge of these problems, attending all public meetings dealing with community issues, and having a personal stake in our communities. We must own and control our communities! By allowing others to control Black communities, we have suffered severely. These entities have given us inadequate housing, under performing schools, unhealthy food choices, and zero to low chances for economic opportunity which has led to our future generations feeding the system but not adding to the value of Black people.

We begin to see how all of these issues are connected and play a larger role in the reasons Black people are in the position we are in. All of these short comings play a valuable economic role in the maintaining of America by feeding the world's largest prison system that is mainly used to house Black people for non-violent offenses. Once we understand how allowing others to control our environment will serve their needs and not our own, and we identify, mobilize and organize our people who want to create change, we will begin to act in the best interest of Black people.

1. What are your beliefs about affordable housing for the Black community in your city/county/parish?

_____

_____

_____

_____

_____

_____

Public Housing Authority/ Misuse of Funds

The public housing authority's mission is to provide affordable housing options and promote education and economic self-sufficiency through the public system with publicly allocated tax dollars for the residents in a specific geographic area. In large cities such as Houston, the State of Texas provides affordable housing for 58,000 low-income Houstonians, with no adequate programming or viable, meaningful, and realistic avenues for them to improve their situations and exit public housing projects.

Without being knowledgeable of the system and how it works, everything will appear to be running efficiently but they are often misusing public funds. These actions do not serve the Black community and hurt our communities physically through the purchase of contaminated land and other harmful dealings. These decisions are made without the knowledge of the majority of the community and benefits multiple parties except for the party it is supposed to serve, the city's low-income residents. These agencies have been operating on a need to know basis and, as a result, it takes multiple actions to release information that would bring any awareness to their actions. These agencies have abandoned their own mission of making residents self-sufficient to allow for an exit of the public housing system, instead it has been a lifelong sentence of depending on government assistance.

It has been found that public housing funds have been used on overpriced, contaminated property and the brokering of deals to line the pockets of the politicians and associates in charge. Everyone concerned citizen being a part of the process is key to holding our elected leaders accountable for the illegal and immoral actions made with public funds. The misuse of public fund is punishable by up to 4 years in state prison and a fine of up to $10,000. Offenders of these crimes have often gotten off with no charges by using the defense such as "lack of criminal intent" or "negligence" or that the "misappropriated funds were incidental and minimal;" therefore, the defendant should not be prosecuted according to the law.

These misappropriations are happening in most low-income, Black communities and hinders our ability to carry out sustainable programs to help Black communities. Tax dollars are instead used to enrich the leadership in power and the businesses they deem acceptable. Demanding transparency of how tax dollars are spent is key to holding our elected officials accountable for all expenditures and ensures that they are being properly allocated toward programs and problems that we deem and approve as acceptable.

We must identify, interview, and run our own candidates to make the systemic transformations we desire. Just because candidates are Black, does not guarantee they will serve our communities in the best way possible.

Zoning Laws

Zoning determines how property in specific geographic areas can be used and details specifically what is acceptable in residential or commercial spaces. Zoning may also regulate lot size and placement as well as the density and height of building structures. Zoning has historically been used as a tool to control large populations of low-income residents by restricting affordable housing and other measures that is used to attract low-income residents. Zoning has been used to restrict good, educational choices by limiting housing choices in area's they want to keep Black people out of.

As a result, our communities are more segregated than ever before. Housing and education policies are treated as separate by policy makers but although they are intertwined, school officials have traditionally drawn school district lines according to the neighborhood boundaries and assign students to schools by their home address. It has been used to section off communities and create a barrier between races, income levels, and other systemic stereotypes. Cities have built major highways to corral and/or section off Black communities to isolate us in areas they can control that also restricts access to funding and other components to building and having a successful community. We must understand the process and who controls the process of making the decisions that affect our communities.

In order to hold elected officials accountable for the lack of progress being made, we must learn to use the same tools of other communities to benefit our people in the future. Zoning often determines your quality of life, the health of your family, and discriminatory policies to deny Black families from basic needs. Before the Fair Housing Act of 1968, federal subsides, tax incentives, and racialized zoning encouraged investments in white only suburbs. Local laws systematized residential segregation through redlining and racial covenants thereby eliminating mixed race public housing. These are simply a few more examples of our Black communities are controlled by outside entities and how Black people end up in a worse state or condition. This should further prove in order for us to get the outcome we desire we must control the people and decisions being made on our behalf. Zoning laws are simply a tool to aid the community and set guidelines for building, but in the wrong hands it can and has been used to suppress, oppress and marginalize Black neighborhoods/communities.

Community Reinvestment Act/Redlining

The Community Reinvestment Act was enacted in 1977 to prevent redlining and to encourage banks to help meet the credit needs of the community including low-income and moderate neighborhoods and individuals. This act was intended to provide the framework for financial institutions and state/ local governments to work within Black communities. Instead, elected officials have used terms like "minority" to exclude Black people from programs that were initially created to counteract systemic & systematic racism. The word "minority" includes many races/groups other than Black people like Asians, Hispanics, Native Americans, and White women, as well as many other sub-racial groups.

The minority title has not helped Black people as a whole but select groups and individuals that knew and know how to maneuver the system. This law (and laws like it) has been used as a tool against Black people by checking off the "minority" box without those in charge being held accountable for exclusive Black participation. Real estate is one of the best ways to build wealth in the united states and it has mainly benefitted other races, while denying Black people access to the same wealth building opportunities with federal law (*The Color of Law By: Richard Rothstein*).

Today's ongoing displacement, exclusion, and legal segregation measures continue to prevent Black people from obtaining and retaining their own homes and access to safe and affordable housing.

Violators of our communities are put into office by our vote; therefore, we must identify individuals that need to be replaced for not initially and repeatedly acting in the best interest of Black people. Every attempt to help Black communities that has been implemented by other people has fallen short for decades and we have continued to rely on the same political process controlled by a system that is dependent on our communities being disorganized and in chaos.

As a result, we will never implement the kinds of programs to bring about revolutionary change until we seek the power required to change it. We must organize around the issues of all Black people and communities and not just seek reformation that gives us the illusion of change in the form of symbolism that changes nothing.

The process of developing a solution for our communities to be economically independent has to be created by and for

Black people and policies we want implemented must be given to the politician(s) by the people they serve and not the other way around.

We must look behind any policy being implemented in our communities and investigate the good and the bad, and who is delivering that policy to us. The solution to these issues is control over the policy making and the person delivering those policies on our behalf.

Restrictions For Public Housing

Public housing was established to provide decent and safe rental housing for eligible low-income families, the elderly, and persons with disabilities. Over decades, the government has set the environment for these housing projects to be the epicenter of crime, drugs, joblessness, lack of opportunity, teenage pregnancy and inadequate education, thereby creating a generational wasteland for Black families and communities.

The low requirements for public housing create negative incentives for families to spend a lifetime and multiple generations within one housing project without ever receiving the tools or education to do and have better. Housing projects serve as breeding grounds for the next generation of juvenile convicts that eventually turn into adult prison inmates.

Large numbers of Black families are forced to live-in low-income neighborhoods because of discriminatory rules against children, lending discrimination from banks and other mortgage lenders, and other restrictions like credit and unusually high income requirements or even disabilities. We are controlled by discriminatory practices because we do not own where we live. Therefore, the policies passed will always serve the needs of others and will never add to the empowerment of Black people. Once we gain our own economic and political power, we will be in the position to hold individuals accountable for policies we disagree with and add policies of our own that will serve our communities as a whole.

What Do We Need To Do?

Community housing for Black people is an issue in every city in this country. We suffer from discriminatory public policies all over the united states and we experience lower home values and lose millions of dollars in equity. Redlining and other legalized housing discrimination practices, the misuse of public tax dollars for personal gain and the criminalization and over policing of Black housing projects all aid in the destruction of our economic hope as a people. We must understand the levers that control the communities that we live in and how to make sustainable change and not fall for temporary solutions by examining actions from the past. To have a successful Black community is to control every aspect of how we live. We must hold elected officials accountable for their inaction, and also take a personal stake in owning every facet of our community to better guarantee a positive outcome for our people. We must introduce programming to help Black resident get out of public housing, eliminate their dependence on government assistance, and empower them to have ownership of their community. We must own the land and the representation of where we live in order to ensure the outcomes we want and expect.

1. Which municipal department is over community/affordable/public housing and how does it work (IS…it working) in your city/county/parish?

_____

_____

_____

_____

_____

_____

2. Is there a specific local politician who has more power/control over this area than others and can a meeting with him/her be scheduled to get more information about their plans, strategies, successes, and failures to date?

_____

_____

_____

_____

_____

3. When does this department meet and how can you learn more about what they're doing to help fix this problem?

_____

_____

_____

_____

_____

4. What municipal department is over zoning laws, who heads this department and how does it work in your city/county/parish?

_____

_____

_____

_____

_____

5. What municipal department is over the community reinvestment act, who heads this department and how does it work in your city/county/parish? Have their strategies/programs been successful or not?

_____

_____

_____

_____

_____

6. Per the opening question for this section and what you've just learned from reading it, can you do more to assist the Black community in this area? If so, in detail, what can you do?

_____

_____

_____

_____

_____

Action Steps

Identify Elected Officials

1. Identify all elected officials that vote on or write laws/amendments to matters dealing with community/public housing.

Identify Public Housing Agencies

2. Identify all public agencies involved with public housing and policies. (Ex: Public Housing Authorities)

Property/Landowner's

3. We must know who owns the land in our communities, both residential and commercial.

4. We must build a relationship with Black housing developers and real estate professionals to begin to partner and buy back our neighborhoods.

Community Engagement/Politics

Community engagement is the process of working with groups of people affiliated by geographic proximity, special interest, or similar situations to address issues affecting the well-being of those people. As history has shown us, politics alone is not the sole solution to helping the Black community but should be used locally as a tool to assist in the goals of our community.

Organizing around an agenda for Black people will help us hold elected officials accountable for every decision they make on behalf of the community. As a part of community engagement, we must demand transparency of city official's detailed budget of expenditures, identify and amend city charters and ordinances that don't serve our Black communities and demand frequent updates from local elected officials on issues/ solutions so we can be proactive instead of reactive when things happen that we do not like or agree with.

Accountability only happens when the community is involved in the process, engaged in the local politics of their neighborhood, and organized around key issues that affect/plague our community. Elected officials make decisions without the accountability of the majority of the

Black community and so they do not feel beholden to act on the behalf of the community.

There must be consequences for acting against the best interest of the Black community and once this is achieved anyone acting outside of the Black community's approval or best interest will be replaced with someone we deem fit to make the right decisions.

We must understand that only through collective organization will we be strong enough to take on these problems and that no individual goal is more important than the shared mission of the group. We have been misled to believe that individual accomplishments will suffice in place of the collective mission of the Black race, but that is false. Each race of people only wields power through the collective power of a larger group and the power of each individual would not be possible without it. We tend to focus on larger political races like the presidency, which we hold little power of affecting major change with, when we should instead focus on local elections that control the way we live our everyday lives. We must examine the powers of local elected officials and how we exert our energy to affect change in the city or state we live in. We overlook the power of the mayor, city council, judges, district attorneys, and other key positions that, instead of protesting or along with protesting, we rally that leverage around a single candidate or platform and empower them to get the answers we are looking for and the solutions we need. If we are really seeking change it cannot be done alone. We must find like-minded Black individuals, groups, or organizations to begin to organize as one to seek the power for future generations.

1. What are your beliefs/thoughts about the how the Black community is engaged politically and with other community focused groups in your city/county/parish?

_____

_____

_____

_____

_____

_____

Detailed City Council Budget/Expenditures

Every city spends millions of our tax dollars on projects that do not benefit the Black community, does not include Black businesses, or does not address any of the issues that face the Black community in a sustainable way.

These issues continue even when Black elected officials are in place. This mere fact should tell us that just electing Black people to office is not the complete and entire key to solving our problems. Simply having a Black elected official in office does not guarantee that person will have a plan to help Black people instead of "Minority" individuals. These elected officials continuously make decisions based on popular talking points that do not help our communities.

We must demand detailed reports of how taxpayer dollars are allocated and spent. For example, each city council member has a budget to allocate towards the district they serve, but at the end of each year, we cannot identify any sustainable changes that have been made. Each year millions of dollars are spent without much of the Black community being aware of where those dollars are going or have the power to hold elected officials accountable for not using those funds appropriately. As citizens we are entitled to know how our tax dollars are spent and it is our responsibility to hold our elected officials accountable for the lack of progress at the end of each year. The elected officials that handle these tasks are elected to office by us, their constituents so; therefore, we should set guidelines and goals for them to accomplish what's needed, required and desired in our communities.

Politicians have spent decades in office without any accomplishments, just superficial accolades. These persons talk but are without real action toward sparking the environment for the development of Black businesses, without real action toward having community update meetings to inform the community on issues we can be proactive, and without real action on changing the products of the system, our people and communities, that needs revolutionary transformation. Only through the power of collective organization and partnership between Black people can we gain the necessary power to control our local politics and the representative that run/control them.

City Charters

A city/county/parish charter is a municipal document that defines the organization, powers, functions, and essential procedures around the governance of that entity. government. Most cities in America are ran by a mayor and city council members that are elected by the people. Over time, when controversial decisions need to be made, elected officials often hold up the status quo that will not affect their future plans of being a career politician.

Politicians have continuously chosen their careers over the will and forward progress of the people and as a result, the Black community suffers from harmful policies and a lack of funds to address and solve ongoing issues. One way to bring about change is a revised or updated city/county/parish charter, which was established by local legislation forming rights and privileges under the local governmental system. In most cases, the municipality's charter can be changed by a vote of the people by referendum vote, which means the people can vote for changes that elected officials would have to write into law.

We can amend the city charter to fit the needs of the people rather than constantly and continuously spending our tax dollars on programs that have failed the community for decades. We must propose measures that put a check on the powers of elected officials and holds them accountable for the decisions they make that harm the community.

Every voting cycle there are city charter amendments being proposed, but these changes treat the symptom of a bigger problem as opposed to the source of the problem. We need transformative amendments of municipal charters on the ballot to make the changes that will make a difference in the Black community. In some cities, amendments only make it to the ballot through the acceptance of the mayor and if we are not organized as a people we cannot gather the power to make the changes to put us in the position to succeed.

Transform City Ordinances

A city ordinance is a law enacted by a municipal body such as a city council or county commission. They govern specific matters not already covered by state or federal laws such as zoning, safety, and building regulations. The power of local government to enact ordinances is derived from the state constitution, statutes or the legislative grant of a municipal charter. The charter dictates the powers of elected officials to regulate actions within the city and an ordinance can only be challenged if it conflicts with state or federal law. Ordinances includes rules for business industries, public safety, equal rights, police and fire protection, public utilities, taxation, water and sewers, and many other key sections to governing a city.

We must seek to pass ordinance amendments that address the root of housing issues, community policing matters, economic opportunity, and other ways that build Black power. Amending city ordinances can eliminate clear conflicts of hiring and firing of leaders that do not carry out the duties of their jobs according to what the community desires, city ordinances can put an end to qualified immunity that allows police to get away with killing unarmed Black people by amending the contract between the city and the police department. This process can work as checks and balances for city and government employees and change procedures to make positions like police chief a publicly elected position. These actions make it easier to hold elected officials accountable when police brutality is not addressed appropriately, by putting their jobs in jeopardy. We must begin to use the system in ways that serve Black people's needs and interests, holds individuals accountable and exercises our right and power as a force in this country. Power does not happen by accident; city ordinances and other tools should be used to aid Black communities. The only way to utilize those tools are to unite as one for our common vision, mission and goals.

Community Accountability/Updates

Elected officials make crucial decisions on behalf of the community without any process to filter the information to the community. Instead, they pass amendments hoping not to receive any public attention and potential outrage. We must hold our elected officials accountable for inclusive planning, transparency, authentic intent, community participation, informed participation, accessible participation, appropriate process, authentic use of information received, feedback to participants, and evaluation of the process and future engagement. These are just a few steps we can take to hold our elected officials accountable and ensure information gets to the community in a timely manner. We must clarify public engagement principles, establish accountability measures for local officials to engage with the community, and evaluate the results of accomplishments based on what the community has laid out. Each elected official should have, at a minimum, quarterly community engagement meetings to bring information back to the community so we can be proactive instead of reactive when issues/problems arise. Having frequent community meeting will serve as an accountability measure for politicians that are not active in our communities, allow us to get to know our representatives, and offer support on issues that may not have support on a state or federal level. Politicians have inhabited our Black communities for decades without having community meetings to inform the community of harmful issues, they have zero accomplishments that have moved Black people forward as a whole and can be sustainable by the community. We must be aware of all the things they are voting for and against, to ensure we are being accurately represented.

At the end of each year, we must have an elected official score card that shows what each person voted for and how it help or hurt the Black community. We have been looking at things backwards by putting on the responsibility on the politician to bring the plans to help Black people, when in reality, it's on us, the community, to bring them the plans we expect to see for our forward progress and advancement. This has created a false sense of reality that the politician has the answers to the issues facing Black people when they are merely products of the system and strive to maintain the same behaviors that set us apart and back. By running our own candidates, we can set proper expectations and explain that they are there to carry out initiatives do a job and not to become a career-politicians while also carrying out initiatives that serve our Black communities.

Monetize and Empower Community Groups

Every community around the nation has local community groups often times referred to as civic associations or super neighborhoods. These groups are usually made up of individuals within a certain geographic area. Their duties are to assist city officials on key issues within that specific geographic area. Historically, these groups have operated without being funded and, as a result, resident participation has been minimal, or members of the community do not know that the group exists. Lack of funding is one reason that prevents these groups from having the proper tools to operate.

They are usually missing key tools to get the appropriate exposure to get others involved such as websites or social media avenues. These groups lack the ability to reach out to the residents for more community participation. This could be solved in most cities by first partnering with groups in Black communities or by each city council member dedicating a portion of its budget to the area they serve to ensure local groups are operating efficiently.

We must guarantee that our tax dollars are funding areas that serve our Black communities; however, to hold elected officials accountable, we must build on our collective power. Depending on others to fund our organizations has never given us the type of programming that solves the issues of Black people, we must be involved in every aspect of our local communities and they need our time as well as our dollars. We must seek to work with local groups that are seeking the advancement and empowerment of Black people to gain control of our communities.

What Do We Need To Do?

Community engagement means being involved in your local community, giving your time and dollars to those who deserve it, holding elected officials and other leaders accountable for doing their job in our communities, investigating methods to improve the city charter and city ordinances by using them as a tool for our benefit, acquiring community updates from our local representatives on a frequent basis, and joining or partnering with grassroots organizations to empower Black people.

There are several things we can do as individuals to be more accountable in our own communities and become more aware of the things taking place around us. We must first be proactive instead of reactive when a situation, issue, or problem arises that threatens our way of life.

1. What elected official or department is responsible for maintaining the city's/county's/parish's budget and how are those funds voted on for distribution?

    _____

    _____

    _____

    _____

    _____

2. How many Black Owned Business are in your city/county/parish and are they represented in the way of municipal contracts? What politician spoke of this during their campaign run and are they doing what they said they would? Who ran against them and why?

    _____

    _____

    _____

    _____

    _____

    _____

3. What are the allocated dollars for the neighborhood where you live and are some of those dollars being allocated for Black people/children?

_____

_____

_____

_____

_____

_____

4. What the process for changing your city's/county's/parish's charter? What IS your municipality's charter?

_____

_____

_____

_____

_____

5. What municipal office/department is responsible for business contracts, public safety, equal rights, police and fire protection, public utilities, taxation, water and sewer?

_____

_____

_____

_____

_____

6. How is a city ordinance created and changed? What's the process for doing this and how difficult is it?

_____

_____

_____

_____

_____

_____

7. What processes exist to hold an elected official accountable in your city/county/parish?

_____

_____

_____

_____

_____

8. What Neighborhood, Community or Civic Association/Organization exists for your specific neighborhood? How often do they meet and is membership easy?

_____

_____

_____

_____

_____

9. Per the opening question for this section and what you've just learned from reading it, can you do more to assist the Black community in this area? If so, in detail, what can you do?

_____

_____

_____

_____

_____

_____

Action Steps

Join Local Groups

1. We must connect with all groups seeking to help the Black community. Only through organization can we begin to seek the power to take back our communities. We must be involved in the economics, education, politics, justice system, community health, agriculture, and structures that promote unity and nation building within Black communities.

Identify Local Elected Officials

2. We must identify our local city officials that make decisions in the communities we live in, research if they are engaged in the community they serve and how often they have community engagement meetings.

Economic Development Opportunity

Economic development and opportunity are the processes whereby low-income national economies are transformed to benefit the communities within the specific geographic area where they operate.

Currently, Black people as a whole, have been left out of the economic prosperity in every major city, in every state in the united states and perhaps the world. Black people have been excluded from land ownership and acquired equity for decades. This provided generations of white families to obtain economic empowerment via the owning of their own property. Furthermore, these discriminatory practices were enforced by federal policies referred to as racial covenants. Racial covenants subjugate large populations into designated ghettos and dilapidated housing projects that turned most of the population into lifetime renters. Economic opportunity is still being denied toward the majority of the Black community.

According to a disparity study completed in Houston, a city dominated by Black elected officials with a Black mayor, Black state representatives, Black senators, and other key positions and Black businesses only acquired .5% of the contracts given from 2016 to 2019. City contracts include construction, landscaping, janitorial work, plumbing, electrical, transportation, and many other categories where Black people have ownership. Black communities have limited economic opportunity. Policies like redlining has excluded Black communities from small business loan programs and investment opportunities, disregarded us from city contract opportunities, disqualified from taking advantage of tax credits for opening new businesses in our communities, and many other economic empowerment tools that could be used to create opportunity in our communities. Increasing the economic opportunity has been proven to lower the crime rate in communities because no individual wants to break the laws for small amounts of return and risk their freedom, but when you are fighting for survival, people will resort to whatever means that has the greatest potential to give them the best foreseeable outcome.

We have discussed how all of our problems as Black people serve the economic empowerment of others, and when we allow others to develop the policies that is supposed to solve that problem, they seem to always fall short. We must solve these issues for ourselves by organizing around the problems that only affect Black people and addressing the root of the issue by holding our elected officials accountable, taking personal accountability for the community around us, and elevated the Black community as our number one priority.

1. What are your beliefs about economic development opportunities for the Black community in your city/county/parish?

_____

_____

_____

_____

_____

_____

Small Business Loan Programs

Many cities have programs, business classes, and various other options that aid minority businesses designed to give information on business solutions and processes, contracting with the city and, in some cases, access to funding. These programs have been flawed because they fail to reach the majority of Black business owners with a sufficient plan to aid them as well as providing a lack of funding sources that would allow their business to adequately compete in the market. Black businesses lack a consistent source of funding from banks, public programs, and other funding mechanisms, but we've had no issues finding loans for homes, cars, and student loans that accumulate debt, but doesn't feed into the economic wealth within our community.

We must hold these programs accountable for their lack of action in Black communities specifically and the amount of tax dollars that is intended to be dedicated to our communities per year. The "minority status" moniker has been used as a weapon against Black people by including other ethnic groups such as American Indians and Alaska Natives, Asians and Pacific Islanders, Hispanics, and white women. This causes Black people to specifically be excluded and discriminated against by using the title "minority" without ever specifying the amount of Black people receiving the benefits. As a result, Black people are systematically left out of programs designed to counteract centuries of economic oppression. We must demand strict requirements and set obligations on funding Black businesses and hold politicians accountable for meeting these standards. This will give elected officials guidelines and expectations of what areas we want to be addressed. We must have programs that look beyond the normal restrictions of loaning funds like credit score, personal assets to leverage, initial seed money, time in business, and eligible business industries.

These are restraints used as a line of defense between black economic empowerment and the structures put in place to increase the disparities within our communities. To really help Black business funding it must be based on having a rock-solid business plan, modest budget of startup, and a plan to reach your target market for your product or service. This will limit the traditional barriers that have been manipulated to keep Black people in a second-class position and promote a lack of ownership of our own communities.

Government/City Contracting

City and government contracting, and procurement is the process by which local governments advertise contracts of work that the city needs completed. A disparity study for the City of Houston was conducted by "Colette Holt & Associates" in 2020 that analyzed all county contract data for all departments from 2016 to 2019, they analyzed 478 contracts given out by the City totaling a net amount of $1,260,717,228 to prime contractors.

Sub-contractors received 1,433 contracts amounting to $280,495,121, and with over 2,000 contracts granted by the City of Houston, Black businesses only accounted for .5%. Black businesses were left out of the contracting process by using the minority status to identify eligible businesses. A method we have verified to work against Black people. This process has allowed Black businesses to be used for acquiring contracts (checking all the right "Minority" boxes) then to only be tossed aside after the contract is granted without any compensation to the Black business or accountability for the parties remaining on the contract. For example, the City of Houston allows prime contractors to select from a list of qualified Black businesses to acquire a city contract to meet their minority business requirement but does not regulate the process after the contract has been granted which in result allows businesses to be used but not participate in the economic advantages.

Small businesses have fought this unfair process in courts, but judges refuse to rule that adequate harm to smaller businesses to make a judgement against prime contractors for breaking the initial agreement or the city for lack of enforcement of the requirements to be granted the contract. This flawed process has caused Black businesses to lose millions of dollars in revenue that could contribute to the overall wealth of our communities. This is not an isolated issue but something Black people are experiencing all over the nation and no one is being held accountable for the exclusion of Black people from economic inclusion.

We must demand full transparency of yearly data of Black business participation in city contracting and other economic drivers and hold elected officials accountable for goals not being met. We also must take the time to learn the process and business structures to give city entities no excuses for the lack of Black business participation.

Tax Abatements

The tax abatement program was created to encourage new growth, developments, and jobs. It was also created to reduce or eliminate property tax for new construction rehabilitation or major improvements. Unfortunately, elected officials have used this incentive to attract business outside of the community that does not aid the economic future of the Black community. Our elected officials have used this program in ways that hurt that Black community and increases their own personal bottom lines. Instead of using these programs to help businesses within that community, it is dangled as a carrot to large companies from outside the community.

These businesses usually offer minimum wage positions with no room for advancement or job growth, it ultimately has no economic future for its employees and often no health benefits. This makes our mission of economic opportunity more difficult in our own communities and locks us out of business ownership by taking up valuable real estate that could have been awarded to a Black business from within. However, tax abatements are given away to large corporations that offer us zero economic inclusion.

When companies receive tax abatements, they are required by law to create a certain amount of jobs specified per state, a detailed financial pro forma from the developer that explains all costs and projected revenue in line-item detail, and minimum investment requirements. We must demand full transparency on everyone receiving tax abatements in our communities. This will allow us to hold companies accountable for tax abatement requirements expressed in their contract. Transparency would also allow us to identify which elected official has granted access to companies outside the community instead of finding businesses from within to benefit from the same opportunities. These are the questions that need to be asked and elected officials should provide the answers if it is not already public knowledge.

Management District/TIRZ

Management districts were created by the legislature to empower, promote, develop, encourage, and maintain employment commerce, transportation, housing, tourism, recreation, arts, entertainment, economic development, safety, and public welfare in a defined area. The few and far between Black communities that can take advantage of the management district structure are ran by members that do not act in the best interest of our communities and look to enrich themselves.

We must demand that contracts first be offered to Black businesses within the community, and full transparency on how public funds are being spent to ensure Black businesses are getting their fair share of tax dollars. We must ensure we are included in the planning and development within our communities that these structures control and are usually appointed by the mayor and city council which should be a conflict of interest.

Anyone making decisions on our communities should be elected by the people of that community. This can be changed by most city/county/parish charters. It has the ability to amend how positions are selected and redirect the power in the hands of the people. The management district is responsible for coordinating resources to effectively manage the community and accomplish objectives established by management and by not being elected by the community, they do not serve the community or accept community input. We can only hold individuals accountable by gaining power in our local communities and that is done by organizing around key issues. We must identify our city/parish council person or district representative that has direct access to what goes on in our community and what decisions they make on behalf of the community ask the questions about if these decisions help or hurt the Black community.

Opportunity Zones

Opportunity zones are tax incentives to encourage those with capital gains to invest in low-income and undercapitalize communities. This program has been a perfect example of a program that does not address the root cause of our communities but exacerbates the disparity of economic inclusion within the Black community. Instead of seeking local businesses to award these opportunities, the program largely attracts large, outside businesses looking to move into a community and pay little to no taxes, while only offering minimum wage jobs.

We must become knowledgeable of our local processes to take advantage of tax credits for serving our communities. Opportunity zones allow business to do business tax free depending on the length of time they have their investment within a community they deem low income or economically deprived or disadvantaged. By definition, this describes that majority of Black communities more than any other race, and as a result, our communities are flooded with businesses of other races and, as a result, they leave Black people in a position to give our dollars to individuals that give nothing back to our community.

In large part, programs like "opportunity zones" has benefitted everyone except the Black communities it was intended to help. Furthermore, we have failed to participate in the tax cuts because it was not created for us. We have discussed whenever a policy is made for us and not by us, it never serves the purpose it is intended to. Once we choose our candidates, they will have an obligation to push the policies we propose, written in a way that permits Black participation.

What Do We Need To Do?

We must advocate for more accountability for small business loan programs, fair city contract processes, take advantage of tax abatements and opportunity zones, create or control our local management district organizations as well as redirect the opportunity zone program to fit our needs. We must begin to spark economic growth within our own communities by buying Black exclusively in spaces where we have a large amount of Black businesses and owning and controlling the key industries that all Black people must patronize. We must create more spaces for trustworthy and fair business partnerships to create business in key industries to take back in our communities, we can co-partner a business, invest in a Black business that is already operating as a start-up, or look to start industries where there is none. We must no longer seek to only have a job but use the job for a reason, season, or purpose and begin to bring that knowledge back to serve Black communities. Control of local economics is the key to our power for education that serves us, protecting ourselves from corrupt justice system practices, gaining political power, expressing our spiritual freedom, and the key to our power as Black people.

1. How many Black Owned Banks and/or Credit Unions exist in your city/county/parish and should there be more?

_____

_____

_____

_____

_____

2. IF you live in a predominantly Black area, how many of the day to day businesses (convenience store, mini-mart, gas station, grocery store, etc.) are owned by a Black person? If you DON'T live in a predominantly Black area, visit one take a survey.

_____

_____

_____

_____

_____

3. What Minority, Small Business Loan Programs exist in your city/county/parish that can benefit Black owned businesses?

_____

_____

_____

_____

_____

_____

4. What municipal office controls government contracting and what politician serves on that/those committees?

_____

_____

_____

_____

_____

_____

5. Is there a process in your city/county/parish to obtain full transparency of yearly data of Black business participation in city contracting and other economic drivers?

_____

_____

_____

_____

_____

6. What municipal department is over tax abatements, how do they work in your city/county/parish and are those funds being used most effectively to benefit the Black community?

_____

_____

_____

_____

_____

7. What municipal department is over management districts/TIRZ, how do they work in your city/county/parish and are those funds being used most effectively to benefit the Black community?

_____

_____

_____

_____

_____

8. Per the opening question for this section and what you have just learned from reading it, can you do more to assist the Black community in this area? If so, in detail, what can you do?

_____

_____

_____

_____

_____

Action Steps

Business Partnership/Black Co-op

1. We must identify high volume businesses in the Black community that we do not own and seek to create a competing business. This will allow us to take the dollars from the business and reinvest in our communities that others do not. We cannot afford for money to leave our communities without investing back.

Identify Elected Officials

2. We must identify local officials who have a budget to dedicate towards the community and hold them accountable for how it is allocated. They have information on large projects taking place in Black communities and we should hold them accountable for Black participation on all projects within that neighborhood.

Economic Programs

3. Tax abatements, opportunity zones, and loan programs have fallen short to help the Black community gain power and ownership in our own communities. We must research and propose our own programs that serve our needs, while holding the present programs accountable for the lack of progress.

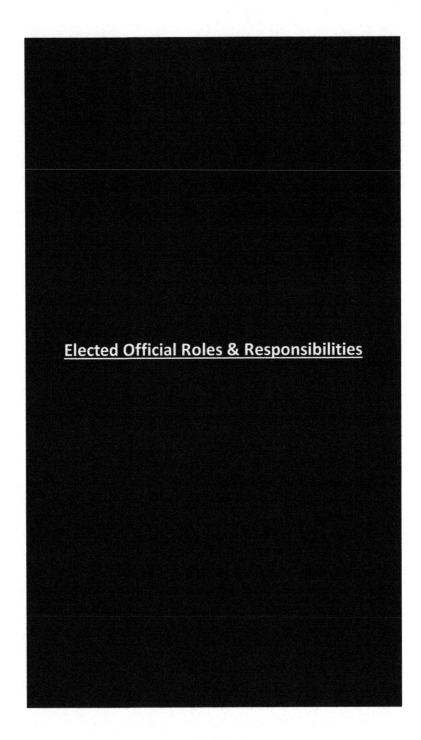

Elected Official Roles & Responsibilities

GOVERNOR

Governors, all of whom are popularly elected, serve as the chief executive officers of the fifty states and five commonwealths and territories. As state managers, governors are responsible for implementing state laws and overseeing the operation of the state executive branch. As state leaders, governors advance and pursue new and revised policies and programs using a variety of tools, among them executive orders, executive budgets, and legislative proposals and vetoes.

Governors carry out their management and leadership responsibilities and objectives with the support and assistance of department and agency heads, many of whom they are empowered to appoint. A majority of governors have the authority to appoint state court judges as well, in most cases from a list of names submitted by a nominations committee.

Although governors have many roles and responsibilities in common, the scope of powers varies from state to state in accordance with state constitutions, legislation, and tradition, and governors often are ranked by political historians and other observers of state politics according to the number and extent of their powers. Ranking factors may include the following. Although not necessarily a ranking factor, the power to issue executive orders and take emergency actions is a significant gubernatorial responsibility that varies from state to state.

- Qualifications and tenure
- Legislative—including budget and veto—authority
- Appointment sovereignty

Qualifications

States, commonwealths, and territories vary with respect to minimum age, U.S. citizenship, and state residency requirements for gubernatorial candidates and office holders. The minimum age requirement for governor's ranges from no formal provision to age 35. The requirement of U.S. citizenship for gubernatorial candidates ranges from no formal provision to 20 years. State residency requirements range from no formal provision to 7 years.

Term Limits

Government terms are four years in every state, commonwealth, and territory but New Hampshire and Vermont, which have two-year terms. All governors with the exception of Virginia's may succeed themselves, although they may be limited to a specific number of consecutive or total terms.

Vacancies/Succession

In the event of a vacancy in office, the lieutenant governor is the designated official who succeeds the governor in 49 states and territories (in two of which—Tennessee and West Virginia—the president/speaker of the Senate and lieutenant governor are one and the same). In the remaining 5 states and the Commonwealth of Puerto Rico, officials designated to succeed the governor include the secretary of state and leader of the senate.

Impeachment

All states except Oregon provide for the impeachment of governors. As in the case of the federal government, the impeachment process starts with the lower body of the legislature and the trial is conducted by the upper body in every state but Alaska—where the process is reversed, and Nebraska, which has a unicameral legislature charged with the full impeachment process.

In most cases, impeachment requires a majority of members, while conviction generally requires a two-thirds or other special majority. Should a governor be impeached, the lieutenant governor serves as acting governor in the vast majority of states.

Appointment Power

Most governors have broad authority to nominate officials to serve in state executive branch positions—many of whom will be included in the governor's advisory committee, known as the "cabinet." Governors may be empowered as well to make appointments to state judgeships. Frequently, these appointments are subject to confirmation by one or both houses of the state legislature. While often pro forma in nature, the confirmation process with respect to executive branch appointments can be used by legislatures to expand their influence on governors and their policies. Accordingly, many governors consult with key legislators before making formal nominations.

Boards and Commissions

The roles played by boards and commissions vary considerably by state and by program. In some states appointed boards have the primary responsibility for individual programs and agencies and are responsible for the selection of department and agency heads. This is particularly true in the field of education, but boards still retain responsibility for a broad range of other programs in fields such as labor, transportation and health and human services. In many states the members of these boards are named or nominated by the governor. And in many of these cases, board members are subject to confirmation by one or both houses of the legislature. Other boards play more limited regulatory or advisory roles. In most states' boards oversee the licensing and regulation of numerous professions and business areas. In other states they advise the governor on areas of importance such as the environment and economic development. While the elimination and/or consolidation of boards and commissions is a common focus of government efficiency and government reorganization initiatives, they still play a prominent role in state government, providing opportunities to address the concerns of special interests and to reward political supporters.

Executive Branch Positions Independently Selected

Many states provide for the independent selection of certain executive branch positions. Most noteworthy among these positions are lieutenant governor, secretary of state, attorney general, and treasurer.

The position of lieutenant governor exists in the overwhelming majority of states, where the position is most often filled by popular statewide election and jointly with the governor, although in a small number of cases the role of lieutenant governor is assigned by state law to another position in either the executive or legislative branch (e.g., secretary of state or leader of the senate). The positions of secretary of state, attorney general, and treasurer are all subject to statewide popular election in most states, and at least one of the three is elected in most of the remaining states.

Governors generally have limited authority in the appointment of state comptrollers and pre and post audit department heads. Governors' appointment powers are also limited with regard to the heads of state education and higher education agencies. The education department head is independently elected statewide in 14 states and is appointed—independent of gubernatorial approval—by a board or agency head in 20 states and two territories. In most states and territories, the higher education head is appointed by a board independent of gubernatorial approval. A number of states also provide for the statewide election of one or more other department heads, among them public utility regulators and the heads of agriculture, labor, and natural resources departments. As with governors, other statewide elected positions may be subject to age, citizenship, and state residency requirements, as well as term limits.

Executive Orders

The authority for governors to issue executive orders is found in state constitutions and statutes as well as case law or is implied by the powers assigned to state chief executives. Governors use executive orders—certain of which are subject to legislative review in some states—for a variety of purposes, among them to:

- Trigger emergency powers during natural disasters, energy crises, and other situations requiring immediate attention.
- Create advisory, coordinating, study, or investigative committees or commissions.
- Address management and administrative issues such as regulatory reform, environmental impact, hiring freezes, discrimination, and intergovernmental coordination.

LT. GOVERNOR

A lieutenant governor may receive responsibilities one of four ways: from the Constitution, from the Legislature through statute, from the governor (through gubernatorial appointment or executive order), through personal initiative in office, and/or a combination of these. The principal and shared constitutional responsibility of every NLGA member is to be the first official in the line of succession to the governor's office.

Lieutenant governors are the only officials with specific duties and powers in two branches of state government: the executive and legislative branches. More than half of the NLGA members preside over their state senate. Most pursue legislative initiatives; many testify locally and in Washington D.C. in various capacities; some serve on the governors' cabinets; and others maintain portfolio of varied duties. The office of lieutenant governor is the most diverse office across state governments. The elected officials of each state and the individual officeholder have the opportunity to utilize the office to most effectively meet the states' unique needs, priorities, and pressing issues.

In many states, the duties of lieutenant governor have been increased by legislation to include the lieutenant governor on state boards, commissions and task forces and to attend to other duties. A lieutenant governor may lead a division, commission, or department of government through gubernatorial or legislative action.

In the states where the official next in line of succession to the governor is a secretary of state or senate president, the responsibilities are those traditionally assigned to the respective office along with the succession and acting governor provisions.

COMPTROLLER

The Comptroller's office serves every citizen in the state. The Comptroller is responsible for many highly technical and critical duties that impacts business owners and individuals all over Texas. The comptroller is the state's chief financial officer. Other important job duties include serving as the chief tax collector, accountant, revenue estimator, treasurer, purchasing manager and checkbook manager for the multi-billion-dollar business of state government. Now let's see some of these duties in more detail.

1. Accountant: The Comptroller is state government's primary accountant, responsible for writing the state's checks and monitoring all spending by state agencies. As the chief accountant, the Comptroller is responsible to ensure the state's financial statements and other reporting requirements are done in accordance with professional accounting principles, rules, and policy.

2. Tax Collector: As the state's chief tax collector, the Comptroller is responsible for collecting more than 60 separate taxes, fees and assessments, including local sales taxes on behalf of more than 1,400 cities, counties

and other local governments. This responsibility includes maintaining taxpayer accounts, processing tax payment exceptions, preparing adjustments, and paying all unclaimed property claims. In addition, the Comptroller's Enforcement Division is responsible for auditing and collecting unpaid taxes owed by businesses.

3. Revenue Estimator: The Comptroller's office is responsible for reporting the state's financial condition to the Legislature annually and providing estimates of revenue for future years. Revenue Estimating monitors and reports on the condition of the state's economy, assists Fiscal Management and Treasury with projecting the state's cash flow position and produces fiscal analyses of legislation, administrative rules and other proposals affecting state revenue.

4. Financial Officer: As guardian of the state's fiscal affairs, agencies depend on the Comptroller's office to pay their bills and issue paychecks to state employees. Legislators rely on the Comptroller to chart the course of the economy, produce annual financial reports and estimate future state revenues. Local officials and businesses look to the agency for economic development guidance and

data analysis. Taxpayers rely upon the agency for assistance and guidance regarding compliance with tax laws. Strict accountability in the collection and expenditure of taxpayer dollars is essential. More importantly, residents depend on the Comptroller's office to account for, manage, and safeguard their tax dollars to ensure they are spent wisely and efficiently.

5. Economic Development: The work of the Comptroller's office does not end there. Turning around and growing Texas' economy is vitally important to the prosperity and quality of life of all in the state. By assisting communities and businesses in their efforts to create new jobs and improve the standard of living, the Comptroller's office is responsible for creating an environment in which a healthy economy can flourish. The agency provides services to business owners, business taxpayers, local officials, Historically Underutilized Businesses (HUBs) and everyday citizens. From online tax data and payment systems to Web pages that track how state government spends taxpayer dollars, the Comptroller's office provides vital information and data.

ATTORNEY GENERAL

The Attorney General is the state's top lawyer and law enforcement official, protecting and serving the people and interests of the state through a broad range of duties. The Attorney General's responsibilities include safeguarding the public from violent criminals, preserving California's spectacular natural resources, enforcing civil rights laws, and helping victims of identity theft, mortgage-related fraud, illegal business practices, and other consumer crimes. Overseeing thousands of lawyers, investigators, sworn peace officers, and other employees, the Attorney General:

- Represents the People of the state in civil and criminal matters before trial courts, appellate courts and the supreme courts of the state and the United States.
- Serves as legal counsel to state officers and, with few exceptions, to state agencies, boards, and commissions.
- Assists district attorneys, local law enforcement and federal and international criminal justice agencies in the administration of justice.
- Strengthens the state's law enforcement community by coordinating statewide narcotics enforcement efforts, supporting criminal investigations and providing

147

forensic science services, identification and information services and telecommunication support.

- Manages programs and special projects to detect and crack down on fraudulent, unfair, and illegal activities that victimize consumers or threaten public safety.

Under the state Constitution, the Attorney General is elected to a four-year term in the same statewide election as the Governor, Lieutenant Governor, Controller, Secretary of State, Treasurer, Superintendent of Public Instruction, and Insurance Commissioner.

LAND COMMISSIONER

A Commissioner General of Lands is an elected position in the state. The holder of this position heads the general land office and serves a four-year term. Some of the duties of the commissioner of general lands include:

- Chairing key state boards and managing mineral rights, state assets and investments.
- The commissioner of general lands has a duty to manage all state-owned land and assets in a way that maximizes revenue.
- He has authority overuse of public land and authorizes professional to explore and exploit it. For example, the commissioner can authorize an energy company to conduct tests on a specific piece of land, determine availability of commercially viable oil and initiate production. Because the commissioner of general lands must balance land use with environmental protection concerns, he develops environmental protection policies that minimize environmental pollution while enhancing land production.

AGRICULTURE COMMISSIONER

In the United States, the agriculture commissioner refers to the head of a state's agriculture department, division, or agency. It is a state-level position within the executive branch of all 50 states. The title and duties of the office vary from state to state, but the general role is to oversee regulation of various facets of the agriculture industry as well as the promotion of state agribusiness.

This state executive office is most commonly appointed rather than elected, with only 12 states using the ballot to select their agriculture commissioners. Besides commissioner, other titles assigned to the role of state agriculture chief include "director" and "secretary" (for example, Iowa Secretary of Agriculture and Missouri Director of Agriculture).

The agriculture commissioner is elected in 12 states: *Alabama, Florida, Georgia, Iowa, Kentucky, Louisiana, Mississippi, North Carolina, North Dakota, South Carolina, and Texas*. The powers and duties of the office vary from state to state, but are often substantial in about 40 states agriculture departments:

- Regulate the animal industry, and in roughly half the states, agriculture departments regulate food safety and meat inspection. In some states, the agriculture commissioner has more power. For example, in Florida the agriculture commissioner is one of three members of the Florida Cabinet (along with the governor and attorney general), giving the commissioner some influence over state policy beyond agriculture. In North Dakota, the agriculture commissioner sits on a number of important boards, such as the North Dakota Industrial Commission (which oversees the state-owned North Dakota Mill and Elevator and Bank of North Dakota).

In the past, these positions were often filled by conservative Democrats, but since 2011 the offices of agriculture commissioners have been dominated by the Republican Party.

SUPREME COURT

In the United States, a state supreme court known by other names in some states is the highest court in the state judiciary of a U.S. state. On matters of state law, the judgment of a state supreme court is considered final and binding in both state and federal courts. Generally, a state supreme court, like most appellate tribunals, is exclusively for hearing appeals of legal issues. Although state supreme court rulings on matters of state law are final, rulings on matters of federal law can be appealed to the Supreme Court of the United States. Each state supreme court consists of a panel of judges selected by methods outlined in the state constitution. Among the most common methods for selection are government appointment, non-partisan election, and partisan election, but the different states follow a variety of procedures.

ROLES & RESPONSIBILITIES

Under the system of federalism established by the United States Constitution, federal courts have limited jurisdiction, and state courts handle many more cases than do federal courts. Each of the fifty states has at least one supreme court that serves as the highest court in the state; two states, Texas and Oklahoma, have separate supreme courts for civil and criminal matters. The five permanently inhabited U.S. territories, as well Washington, D.C., each have comparable supreme courts. On matters of state law, the judgment of a state supreme court is considered final and binding in both state and federal courts. State supreme courts are completely distinct from any United States federal courts located within the geographical boundaries of a state's territory, or the federal-level Supreme Court.

The exact duties and powers of the state supreme courts are established by state constitutions and state law. Generally, state supreme courts, like most appellate tribunals, are exclusively for hearing appeals on decisions issued by lower courts, and do not make any finding of facts or hold trials. They can, however, overrule the decisions of lower courts, remand cases to lower courts for further proceedings, and establish binding precedent for future cases.

Some state supreme courts do have original jurisdiction over specific issues; for example, the Supreme Court of Virginia has original jurisdiction over cases of habeas corpus, mandamus, prohibition, and writs of actual innocence based on DNA or other biological evidence.

JURISDICTION & PROCEDURE

As the highest court in the state, a state supreme court has appellate jurisdiction over all matters of state law. Many states have two or more levels of courts below the state supreme court; for example, in Pennsylvania, a case might first be heard in one of the Pennsylvania courts of common pleas, be appealed to the Superior Court of Pennsylvania, and then finally be appealed to the Supreme Court of Pennsylvania. In other states, including Delaware, the state supreme court is the only appellate court in the state and thus has direct appellate jurisdiction over all lower courts.

Like the U.S. Supreme Court, most state supreme courts have implemented "discretionary review." Under such a system, intermediate appellate courts are entrusted with deciding the vast majority of appeals. Intermediate appellate courts generally focus on the mundane task of what appellate specialists call "error correction, "which means their primary task is to decide whether the record reflects that the trial court correctly applied existing law. In a few states without intermediate appellate courts, the state supreme court may operate under "mandatory review", in which it *must* hear all appeals from the trial courts. This was the case, for example, in Nevada prior to 2014.

154

For certain categories of cases, many state supreme courts that otherwise have discretionary review operate under mandatory review, usually with regard to cases involving the interpretation of the state constitution or capital punishment. One of the informal traditions of the American legal system is that all litigants are entitled to at least one appeal after a final judgment on the merits. However, appeal is merely a *privilege* provided by statute, court rules, or custom in 49 states and in federal judicial proceedings; the U.S. Supreme Court has repeatedly ruled that there is no federal constitutional *right* to an appeal.

COURT OF CRIMINAL APPEALS

To relieve the Supreme Court of some of its caseload, the Constitution of 1876 created the Court of Appeals, composed of three elected judges, with appellate jurisdiction in all criminal cases and in those civil cases tried by the county courts. In 1891, a constitutional amendment:

• Changed the name of this court to the Court of Criminal Appeals.

• Limited its jurisdiction to appellate jurisdiction in criminal cases only.

• Increased the number of judges to nine: one presiding judge and eight associate judges.

The Court of Criminal Appeals is the highest state court for criminal appeals. Its caseload consists of both mandatory and discretionary matters. All cases that result in the death penalty are automatically directed to the Court of Criminal Appeals from the trial court level. A significant portion of the Court's workload also involves the mandatory review of applications for post-conviction habeas corpus relief in felony cases without a death penalty,9 over which the Court has sole authority. In addition, decisions made by the intermediate courts of appeals in criminal cases may be appealed to the Court of Criminal Appeals by petition for discretionary review, which may be filed by the State, the defendant, or both. However, the Court may also review a decision on its own motion.

STATE BOARD OF EDUCATION

State boards of education are different in every state and have diverse policy authority. Some are created by the state constitution and others by statute. Some of their members are elected; some are appointed. In many states, it is the state board who selects the state education chief. In others, it is the governor. In 45 states, the state board adopts learning standards that all students are expected to achieve. In 31 states, state boards have primary authority over state summative assessments. In addition, most SBEs have the following authority:

- Establishing high school graduation requirements.
- Determining qualifications for professional education personnel.
- Establishing state accountability and assessment programs.
- Establishing standards for accreditation of local school districts and preparation programs for teachers and administrators.

Regardless of their level of authority, all boards and board members have three important powers:

(1) authority for **adopting and revising policies** that promote educational excellence and equity,

(2) **convening** experts and stakeholders to serve as a bridge between policymakers and citizens, and

(3) the **power to raise questions** as the citizens' voice in education. State boards leverage these combined powers to act boldly with and for students, educators, and families.

RAILROAD COMMISSION

The Office of the Commissioner of Railroads is the state agency with primary responsibility for making determinations of the adequacy of warning devices at railroad crossings, along with other railroad and water carrier related regulations. These duties include:

- Installation of new highway/rail crossings.
- Alteration of existing crossings.
- Closing or consolidating existing crossings.
- Repair of rough crossings.
- Determining adequate railroad fences.
- Exemptions from railroad track clearance laws.
- Assist with rail safety initiatives and participate in community outreach.

STATE REPRESENTATIVE

A state representative is a politician who serves in a state-level legislative branch. These politicians represent local cities or counties and help to form state laws that benefit their constituents. A career as a state representative is often a steppingstone to future positions with the U.S. Congress or other political jobs at the state or federal level.

State representatives introduce and vote on bills that represent the interests of their constituents (people who live in their voting district):

- They create new laws, modify or update old laws and serve on research committees within the legislative branch.
- These representatives uphold the state's Constitution, and vote on changes to the Constitution when amendments are needed.
- They may address issues such as education, transportation, commerce, state taxes and any other items that are a concern to local residents.
- Representatives may also assist constituents with personal legal issues such as immigration or justice problems.

To serve as a state representative, an individual must be a legal resident of the area he plans to represent. He must be between the ages of 21 and 67 years, though exact age requirements vary by state. State representatives cannot have been convicted of a felony within the 20 years prior to election and may not hold any other political job while they serve in the legislature. Most states elect representatives for 4-year terms, though term limits and duration may vary.

STATE SENATOR

State senators are responsible for representing the interests of the citizens in their district when considering legislation for the state. Their job is to improve the lives of their constituents. As elected officials, state senators are paid servants of the people, but their salaries vary greatly. Senators in Idaho, for example, were paid $16,438, while senators earned as much as $90,526 in California in 2014. The job of a state senator is:

- To create and pass legislation that will benefit the citizens of his or her district, as well as the entire state.
- To do this, state senators must work within their committees and form relationships with senators who have different political views.
- Negotiating is a major part of a state senator's job. They must debate and persuade other senators to support or oppose particular legislation.

State senators represent small populations of citizens compared with U.S. senators, and much of their job consists of:

- Responding to constituents' needs. Many voters contact their state senators to request they vote a certain way for legislation or simply to vent their frustrations.
- As an elected official, the state senator must reply to the needs of the voters and keep them satisfied.
- Some provide monthly or quarterly newsletters to the voters in their district.

MAYOR

Mayor, in modern usage, the head of a municipal government. As such, the mayor is almost invariably the chairman of the municipal council and of the council executive committee. In addition, the mayor may fulfill the roles of chief executive officer, ceremonial figurehead, and local agent of the central government. In another, more recent, system of municipal management the council-manager system the mayor has a much-reduced role, serving essentially only as head of the council. Whatever the form of local government, the mayor's role may be said to rest largely on the relationship of the mayor to the council and to the central government.

These responsibilities may include:

- Serving on the city council.
- Voting in council meetings.
- Assigning council members to chair or serve on committees.
- Appointing citizens to serve on advisory boards or commissions.
- Preparing the annual budget; Receiving the annual budget developed by chief administrative official or city manager.
- Making an annual report to the council.

CITY COUNCIL

The title for the members of city councils vary, and several titles exist according to local custom. These titles are councilmember, alderman, selectman, freeholder, trustee or commissioner. Councils can range in size from 5 to 51 across the nation, although the national average is six. While the number of councilmen is proportional to the population of the municipality, there is no national standard of proportion. In addition, the size of a council may reflect the complexity of services provided, the council's workload, the diversity and size of the population, the political dynamics and preferences of the city. This variability is illustrated by the large range in the number of councilmen per number of constituents, from 6,278 in Albany to over 250,000 in Los Angeles.

As local legislators, councilmembers are responsible for and responsive to the citizens who elected them. Depending on the city's charter and state laws, they may perform the following functions:

- Review and approve the annual budget.
- Establish long- and short-term objectives and priorities.
- Oversee performance of the local public employees.

- Oversee effectiveness of programs.
- Establish tax rates.
- Enter into legal contracts.
- Borrow funds.
- Pass ordinances and resolutions.
- Modify the city's charter.
- Regulate land use through zoning laws.
- Regulate business activity through licensing and regulations.
- Regulate public health and safety.
- Exercise the power of eminent domain.
- Communicate policies and programs to residents.
- Respond to constituent needs and complaints; and
- Represent the community to other levels of government.

CITY CONTROLLER

The City Controller serves as the City's Chief Financial Officer and is responsible for ensuring that the assets of the City are properly accounted for and expended in a manner consistent with applicable laws, policies, plans and procedures. To accomplish this goal, the City Controller performs various functions including but not limited to the following:

- Certifying the availability of City funds prior to Council approval of City commitments,
- Processing and monitoring disbursements which total $2.4 Billion annually,
- Investing the City's funds,
- Conducting internal audits of City departments and federal grant programs,
- Operating and maintaining the City's financial management system,
- Conducting the sale of the City's public improvement and revenue bonds, and
- Producing a comprehensive annual financial report.

COUNTY JUDGE

The county judge is the presiding officer and a voting member of the commissioner's court and constitutional county court. Actual judicial responsibilities of county judges vary among counties because statutory county courts at law exist with overlapping jurisdiction in many counties. In a few counties, portions of usual county court jurisdiction have been assigned to district courts. In many major metropolitan areas, the job of the county judge is primarily administrative rather than judicial in nature. In the role of presiding officer of the commissioner's court, the county judge oversees all county government departments through the court's responsibility for approving annual budgets for the entire county. Generally, county courts have jurisdiction in civil cases when the amount in controversy is at least $200 but not over $10,000. County courts also have jurisdiction in probate matters, appellate (from justice of the peace courts) jurisdiction over Class C misdemeanors, and original jurisdiction in Class A and B misdemeanors. Constitutional county judges have original jurisdiction in probate matters, including mental illness and guardianships. The county judge may act as juvenile judge and serve on the county juvenile board, as well as conduct marriages and act as a coroner, when necessary. A county judge is not required to be an attorney, but the county judge "shall be well-informed in the law of the state."

- Empowered by the Constitution as the County's Chief Executive officer.
- The presiding officer of the Commissioners Court including publishing meeting notices and prohibiting illegal closed meetings.
- Administrative duties primarily relate to carrying out the court orders passed by the Commissioners Court, signing all contracts, and overseeing all non-elected department heads.
- Fort Bend County liaison between State, Federal, City and other County Governments.
- Actively participates in both public and private sector economic development.
- Director of Emergency Management and oversees civil defense and disaster relief for the county residents.
- Serves on the County Bail Bond Board, Purchasing Board, the Juvenile Board and the County Elections Commission.
- As a voting member of the Commissioners Court performs many of the same duties and responsibilities as a County Commissioner.

- Sets and receives bonds or sureties for certain county officials and other appointments by Commissioners Court.
- Refuses or issues Court Ordered Delayed Birth Certificates and Death Certificates.
- Other than the largely administrative duties listed above, all judicial duties of the County Judge are vested in the six County Courts- at- Law maintained by Fort Bend County.

COUNTY COMMISSIONER

County commissioners are a county's key policymakers, overseeing the operation and administration of the county. Commissioners are the elected officials of a county's legislative branch, the County Board of Commissioners, serving in a similar role as a city councilmember or a state representative or senator. Commissioners are responsible for overseeing the county's management and administration, representing county interests at the state and federal level, participating in long-range planning, and managing the county budget and finances.

- Serves, on a rotation basis with the other Commissioners, as Chairman of the Board of Commissioners and in this capacity presides over meeting of the board; assists in the coordination of board responsibilities.

- Acts as a member of the County Budget Committee in the preparation of County budget; estimates and determines amount of revenue required; levies rates necessary for appropriation of funds; supervises all county financing.

- Appoints and employs the County Engineering personnel and assists in the planning and supervision of the construction and maintenance and repair of all county

172

roads and bridges; directs purchase of equipment and rights-of-way.

- Appoints and employs the Director of Parks and Director of Lands and Forests and assists in the planning, supervision and construction of all County Parks, approves or disapproves purchase of land, land exchanges, land leases and timber sales, directs purchase of equipment and contracts for building and/or repairs.

- Approves or disapproves all county purchases, payrolls, contracts, deeds, leases and acquisitions whether real or personal property with the exception of certain business transactions which are taken care of by some departments of county government pursuant to state law.

- Appoints such county boards and commissions as Planning Commission, Dog Control Board, Fair Board, etc.

- Supervises all county property provides for the erection, repair and usage of county buildings.

- Establishes, vacates or alters county roads within the county.

- Grants licenses and controls licenses as authorized by state law.

- Directs expenditure of funds for promotion of county resources including county membership in travel, recreational and industrial organizations.

- From time to time, meets with cities within the county, adjoining counties, state and government officials in matters of coordination, cooperation and matters of policy at various levels of government and for the purpose of agreements relating to land and water uses, cooperative projects, and matters of mutual interest; meets with school boards and various other boards and organizations in matters of local interest.

- Appoints County Health Officer who, in turn, outlines and places in effect a health program as advocated by the State Health Division.

COUNTY ATTORNEY

The County Attorney is to defend the County in all lawsuits; issue civil legal opinions upon request to all elected officials and department heads; prepare and/or review all contracts entered into by the County; and conduct legal research required to assist all county departments; and actively serve as advisors to County officials and department heads and Child Protective Services ("Clients"). Additionally, the office proactively seeks ways to prevent the County and its employees from being exposed to legal actions; efficiently and effectively provides all the civil legal services for the County and certain services for the state, including Child Protective Services; provides effective litigation services; and assures adequate delinquent collections of bail bond forfeitures and unpaid drainage district improvements. The duties and responsibilities of the County Attorney are broadly defined in Section 45.179 of the Government Code.

- Prosecute all violations of state criminal laws and county ordinances.
- Provide legal advice to the Board of Supervisors and county and township officers concerning county matters.
- Represent and defend the state, county, and its officers in officially related cases.

- Recover all monies (debts, fines, penalties, etc.) owing to the state or county.
- Present all mental health commitment proceedings and all juvenile delinquency and child in need of assistance cases.
- In his or her OFFICIAL capacity, the County Attorney is NOT a lawyer for a private group or person.

DISTRICT ATTORNEY

A lawyer who is elected or chosen by local government officials to represent the state government in criminal cases brought in a designated county or judicial district. A DA's duties typically include reviewing police arrest reports, deciding whether to bring criminal charges against arrested people, and prosecuting criminal cases in court. The DA may also supervise other attorneys, called Deputy District Attorneys or Assistant District Attorneys. In some states, a District Attorney may be called a Prosecuting Attorney, County Attorney, or State's Attorney. In the federal system, the equivalent to the DA is a United States Attorney. The country has many U.S. Attorneys, each appointed by the president, who supervise regional offices staffed with prosecutors called Assistant United States Attorneys.

- To attend on the grand juries, advise them in relation to matters of law, and examine and swear witnesses before them.
- To draw up all indictments and to prosecute all indictable offenses.
- To prosecute and defend any civil action in the circuit court in the prosecution or defense of which the state is interested.

- To inquire whether registers have kept accurate required record books.

- If a criminal prosecution is removed from a court of his or her circuit, county, or division of a county to a court of the United States, to appear in that court and represent the state; and, if it is impracticable, consistent with his or her other duties, to attend that court, he or she may designate and appoint an attorney practicing therein to appear for and represent the state.

- To attend each special session of the circuit court held for the trial of persons charged with criminal offenses.

- To perform other duties and exercise other powers as are or may be required by law.

- To give every county official an opinion in writing on all matters connected with their respective offices, except in civil actions against official bonds. But county commissions may retain or employ attorneys when it is deemed advisable or necessary, and the agreed compensation to them may be paid as are claims to grand and petit jurors.

- To, whenever requested to do so by the Governor or by the Board of Pardons and Paroles, make a full and thorough investigation in each case arising in their circuit, county, or division of a county, and fully report their findings, with recommendations that pardon or parole be granted or refused, and they shall assign fully and in detail their reasons for the recommendations.

- To go to any place in the state and prosecute any case or cases, or work with any grand jury, when called upon to do so by the Attorney General or the Governor, and to attend sessions of courts and transact all of the duties of the district attorney in the courts whenever called upon by the Attorney General or the Governor to do so.

- All district attorneys and all full-time assistant district attorneys shall devote their entire time to the discharge of the duties of their respective offices, and each and every one of the officers are prohibited from practicing law, directly or indirectly, in any court of this state or of the United States, or in any other manner or form whatsoever, except in the discharge of the official duties of their offices.

- To carefully read and check the record on appeal in all criminal cases appealed from the circuit court of their judicial circuit to the Court of Criminal Appeals or the Supreme Court of the state and call to the attention of the trial judge any errors or discrepancies that may appear in the record.

- To, whenever requested by the Attorney General, file memorandum briefs in all criminal cases appealed from the circuit court of their judicial circuits to the Court of Criminal Appeals or the Supreme Court of the state.

- To attend all hearings in their judicial circuits on any application for probation and furnish the trial judge or the judge hearing the application with all information in their possession concerning the applicant for probation.

- To represent the board of registrars of the county or counties comprising their judicial circuits in all civil actions for damages that are filed against the boards of registrars arising out of the performance of their official duties, in either the circuit court of their judicial circuits or in the United States district courts.

- To attend all clemency hearings before the Governor of the state, in all cases arising in their judicial circuits, and furnish to the Governor, at those hearings, all pertinent information in their possession concerning the applicant or applicants for clemency.

- To attend all hearings in their respective judicial circuits for revocation of probation and furnish the trial judge, or the judge hearing the revocation, with all information in their possession concerning the case.

- To, at any time the grand jury is not in session, issue subpoenas to persons to come before them, and they shall have power to administer oaths to those persons and examine them as to any violation of the criminal laws of the state.

- To make application to the courts to place witnesses in criminal cases under bond for their appearance in court when they have information that the witnesses are about to leave the state.

- To, when requested to do so, represent the chief of police of any municipality in their respective judicial circuits in all habeas corpus proceedings filed in the circuit courts of their respective judicial circuits.

- To, when requested to do so by the Attorney General, assist the Attorney General in the prosecution of all impeachment proceedings which it is his or her duty to institute before a court involving any official or officials in their respective judicial circuits.

- To report to the State Board of Medical Examiners the name and address of any physician who is indicted or otherwise charged with any felony or any misdemeanor related to the practice of medicine.

COUNTY CLERK

County clerks come in all forms and levels of authority. Some are elected, some are appointed. Some are clerks to the governing board only and others have responsibilities for carrying out many services for the citizens of the county. In California and New York, it is discretionary whether counties elect their clerks or appoint them. Of the remaining states, the role either is an appointed position, or does not exist.

Today, County Clerks are generally responsible for maintaining records of all governing body transactions including resolutions and ordinances. They are responsible for keeping records of deeds and marriage licenses and most other public records. They also issue permits for various parades and parties, as well as many licenses. Another major duty of many elected County Clerks is that of receiving all nominations and petitions for elections. The Clerk also is responsible for preparing ballots, procuring and maintaining voting machines and recruiting and training poll workers and the conduct of all elections.

As an example of the role of the clerk as authorized by law outlines the role of the office as follows:

1. Recorder of the county, on behalf of the Board of County Commissioners

2. Chief election officer responsible for the administration of elections in the

3. Clerk of the Probate Court in handling informal proceedings only

4. Miscellaneous duties including those of notary public, administration of oaths, certification of acknowledgements, declarations, instruments, and protests.

The county clerk is responsible for keeping records, resolutions and ordinances adopted by the Board of County Commissioners. The county clerk also serves as the secretary to the commission and performs all of the following:

- Records all proceedings of the board and makes regular entries of all resolutions and decisions in all questions that concern the raising of money; records the vote of each commissioner on any question submitted to the board.

- Signs all orders issued by the board for payment of money, records the action and records the receipts of the county treasurer that show the income and expenditures of the county.

DISTRICT CLERK

District clerks are called on to assure that the affairs of the district courts are maintained objectively with the full confidence of judicial authorities. The government code states the duties and powers of the clerk district court, the clerk of the district court has custody of and shall carefully maintain and arrange the records relating to or lawfully deposited in the clerk's office.

- Record the acts and proceedings of the district court.
- Enter all judgements of the court under the direction of the judge.
- Record all executions issued and the returns issued on the executions.
- Process passport applications.
- Administer child support payments.
- Administer trust accounts for minors ordered by the courts.
- Keep an index of the parties to all suits filed in the court, and make reference to any judgment made in the case.
- Keep an account of all funds collected by the office, by way of fines and fees, and the amount due jurors in district court for service.

- Manage records so they are easily retrieved for public information, preserved for permanent storage in archives and dispose of according to law.
- Gather data and report to State and Local agencies (County Treasurer, County Auditor, Voter Registrar, Bureau of Vital Statistics, Department of Public Safety, Attorney General, State Treasurer, State Board of Medical Examiners, State Library, Comptroller of Public Accounts and Office of Court Administration)

Be in charge of the jury selection process to determine the number of potential jurors required to begin trial, send summons to jurors, process jurors on trial day, pay jurors for service and act a liaison between the jurors, courts and employers.

COUNTY TREASURER

The county treasurer holds a key position of public trust in the financial affairs of local government. Acting as the bank for the county, school districts, fire districts, water districts, and other units of local government, the treasurer's office receipts, disburses, invests, and accounts for the funds of each of these entities. In addition, the treasurer is charged with the collection of various taxes that benefit a wide range of governmental units.

The major responsibilities of the county treasurer can be summarized in the following areas:

- Receipting and accounting of revenue
- Disbursement of funds
- Collection of taxes
- Cash management
- Debt management

The county treasurer adds value to the taxing districts and citizens by providing:

- Efficiency and expertise in providing county-wide treasury services
- Centralized revenue collection

- Reduction in local government financial service costs to county taxpayers
- Consolidated investment services
- Reduction in banking service cost
- Additional internal controls
- Financial analysis expertise
- Assistance in revenue projections and debt service payments

COUNTY SHERIFF

The sheriff acts as a conservator of the peace and the executive officer of the county and district courts, serve writs and processes of the courts, seizes property after judgment, enforce traffic laws on county roads and supervises the county jail and prisoners. In counties of fewer than 10,000 residents, he may also serve as ex officio tax assessor and collector. The main duties of a sheriff are law enforcement, the courts and the jail. The duties of the sheriff:

- To execute and return the processes and orders of the courts.

- To attend, by himself or his deputy, upon all sessions of the Superior Court of the county and also upon sessions of the Probate Court whenever required, and while the courts are in session, never to leave the same without the presence of himself or his deputy, or both, if required.

- To attend at the place or places of holding an election at the county site, on the day of an election, from the opening to the closing of the polls.

- To publish sales, citations, and other proceedings as required by law and to keep a file of all newspapers in which his official advertisements appear.

- To keep an execution docket wherein he must enter a full description of all executions delivered to him and the dates of their delivery, together with all his actions thereon.

- To keep a book in which shall be entered a record of all sales made by process of court or by agreement of the parties under the sanction of the court, describing accurately the property and the process under which sold, the date of the levy and sale, the purchaser, and the price.
- To receive from the preceding Sheriff all unexecuted writs and processes and proceed to execute the same; to carry into effect any levy or arrest made by a predecessor; to put purchasers into possession, and to make titles to purchasers at his or her predecessor's sales, when not done by his or her predecessor.
- To perform such other duties as are or may be imposed by law or which necessarily appertain to his or her office.
- To exercise the same duties, powers, and arrest authority within municipalities which such officer exercises in the unincorporated areas of counties.
- To develop and implement a comprehensive plan for the security of the county courthouse and any courthouse annex. The sheriff shall be responsible to conduct a formal review of the security plan not less than every four years.

TAX ACCESSOR COLLECTOR

The Tax Assessor-Collector calculates property tax rates for the county, collects taxes for the county (and sometimes for additional local taxing entities) and collects various other fees for the state and county.

1. Calculates property tax rates for the county.
2. Collects property taxes for the county.
3. May collect taxes for cities, schools, and other local taxing entities.
4. Processes motor vehicle title transfers.
5. Issues motor vehicle registration and licenses.
6. May process boat titles and registrations.
7. Registers voters and may conduct elections.
8. Collects various other fees for the state and county.

JUSTICE OF THE PEACE

The Justice of the Peace presides over the justice court in cases involving misdemeanors, small civil disputes, landlord/tenant disputes and more. They also conduct inquests and may perform marriage ceremonies.

1. Hears traffic and other Class C misdemeanor cases punishable by fine only.
2. Hears civil cases with up to $10,000 in controversy.
3. Hears landlord and tenant disputes.
4. Hears truancy cases.
5. Performs magistrate duties.
6. Conducts inquests.

CONSTABLE

A Constable is a licensed peace officer and performs various law enforcement functions. They also serve legal documents and perform other duties.

1. Serves as a licensed peace officer and performs various law enforcement functions, including issuing traffic citations.
2. Serves warrants and civil papers such as subpoenas and temporary restraining orders.
3. Serves as bailiff for Justice of the Peace Court.

COUNTY AUDITOR

The County Auditor countersigns all warrants on the county treasury, examines the treasurer's reports and all claims against the county, advertises for bids on county supplies, and exercises general oversight over the financial books and records of the county.

1. Appointed by the district judge(s).
2. Prepares and administers accounting records for all county funds.
3. Audits the records and accounts of the various county departments.
4. Verifies the validity and legality of all county disbursements.
5. Forecasts financial data for budgetary formulation purposes.
6. Serves as budget officer in counties with more than 225,000 residents (Counties with more than 125,000 residents may opt for an appointed budget officer.)

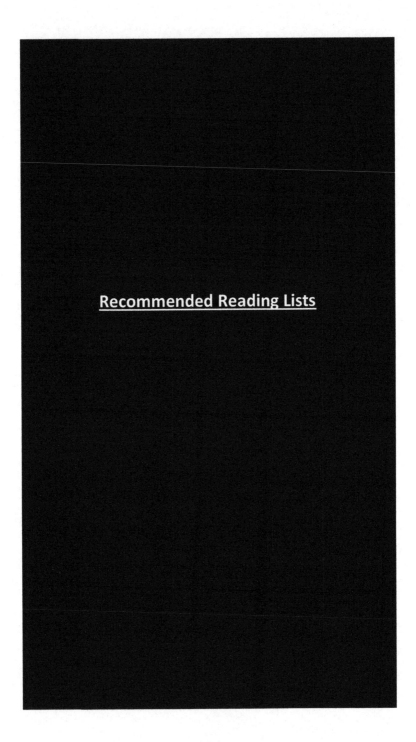

<u>Recommended Reading Lists</u>

- **The New Jim Crow: Mass Incarceration in the Age of Colorblindness** - Michelle Alexander

- **Black Labor, White Wealth** – Dr. Claud Anderson

- **The Black Tax: The Cost of Being Black in America** - Shawn D Rochester

- **Inequalities: Children in America's Schools** - Jonathan Kozol

- **Slavery by Another Name: The Re-Enslavement of Black Americans from the Civil War to World War II** - Douglas A. Blackmon

- **The Color of Law: A Forgotten History of How Our Government Segregated America** - Richard Rothstein

- **Blood at the Root: A Racial Cleansing in America Hardcover** - Patrick Phillips

- **When Affirmative Action Was White: An Untold History of Racial Inequality in Twentieth** - Ira Katznelson

- **Not in My Neighborhood: How Bigotry Shaped a Great American City** - Antero Pietila

- **Under the Affluence: Shaming the Poor, Praising the Rich and Sacrificing the Future of America** - Tim Wise

- **Behold a Pale Horse** - Milton William Cooper

- **The Spook Who Sat by the Door** - Sam Greenlee

- **Black Against Empire: The History and Politics of the Black Panther Party** - Joshua Bloom, Waldo E. Martin Jr.

- **The Color of Money: Black Banks and the Racial Wealth Gap** - Mehrsa Baradaran

- **Economism: Bad Economics and the Rise of Inequality** - James Kwak, Simon Johnson

- **The Looting Machine: Warlords, Oligarchs, Corporations, Smugglers, and the Theft of Africa's Wealth** - Tom Burgis

- **Ego Is the Enemy** - Ryan Holiday

- **Afrikan-Centered Consciousness Versus the New World Order: Garveyism in the Age of Globalism** - Amos N Wilson

- **Awakening the Natural Genius of Black Children 1st Edition** - Amos N. Wilson

- **Black-On-Black Violence: The Psychodynamics of Black Self-Annihilation in Service of White Domination** - Amos N. Wilson

- **The Falsification of Afrikan Consciousness: Eurocentric History, Psychiatry and the Politics of White Supremacy** - Amos N. Wilson

- **Developmental Psychology of the Black Child** - Amos N. Wilson

- **The Development Psychology of the Black Child Paperback** - Amos Wilson

- **Issues of Manhood in Black and White** - Amos N. Wilson

- **The Psychology of Self-Hatred and Self-Defeat: Towards a Reclamation of the Afrikan Mind** - Amos N. Wilson, Sababu N. Plata

- **Blueprint for Black Power: A Moral, Political and Economic Imperative for the Twenty-First Century**
  - Amos N. Wilson